D1200105

1-22

The Complete Guide to Small Group Ministry

The Complete Guide to Small Group Ministry

Saving the World Ten at a Time

Robert L. Hill

Skinner House Books
Boston

Hundreds of Unitarian Universalists who responded to surveys and articles in my e-mail newsletter, *Covenant Group News,* contributed to these chapters and to the brief collection of documents at the end. Many others have shared their insights, concerns, and dreams with me by phone or in person. My thanks both to those I have quoted by name in these pages and to those whose contributions to my understanding of covenant groups and Small Group Ministry are significant but not duly recognized here. I am grateful to my employers, who gave me the gift of writing time when I could have been doing other work. They are the Boards of the Southwestern Unitarian Universalist Conference, including former president Kathy Calhoun and current president Mark Westergard, and, on the UUA side, Dr. Tracey Robinson-Harris, former supervisor of the District Staff, and Peter Morales, who holds that position now. Dr. James Brown, by deciding to move toward retirement and asking me to share his District Executive position, made this book possible. I could not have become so engrossed in covenant group theory and practice without the advantage of two years of half-time employment before my district executive duties became full-time and then some in 2000. My first experience of working with a Skinner House Books editor has given me a new and valuable insight into my own writing: I need a lot more editing than I thought. Mary Benard is thorough, patient, and highly skilled. Finally, I wish to thank a former UUA headquarters staff person who has been the light of my life for more than a decade, Dr. Kristi C. Heesch. I'm indebted to the University of Texas and Oklahoma University for keeping her so busy as a student and then as a professor that she couldn't object to the time this project took from our marriage.

—*Bob Hill*

Copyright © 2003 by Robert L. Hill. All rights reserved. Published by Skinner House Books. Skinner House Books is an imprint of the Unitarian Universalist Association, a liberal religious organization with more than 1,000 congregations in the U.S. and Canada. 25 Beacon Street, Boston, MA 02108.

Printed in Canada

Cover design by Kathryn Sky-Peck. Text design by WordCrafters.

ISBN 1-55896-457-6

Library of Congress Cataloging-in-Publication Data

Hill, Robert L., 1938–
    The complete guide to small group ministry : saving the world ten at a time / Robert L. Hill.
      p. cm.
    ISBN 1-55896-457-6 (alk. paper)
     1. Church group work—Unitarian Universalist Association. 2. Small groups—Religious aspects—Unitarian Universalist Association. 3. Unitarian Universalist Association—Membership. I. Title.

BX9841.H55 2003
253'.7—dc21

2003045485

5 4 3 2
06 05 04

Of what value are the religious scriptures, scrolls, tapestries, regalia, houses of worship, chanting, rituals, meditation, prayers, fasting, slogans, proselytizing, missionaries, donations, and sermons, if they do not produce useful reactions of individuals to individuals? Do they produce the recognition that others need the same respect and justice as we would want? Does the treatment of other people as we would be treated carry over into the workplace, the government, the home, and the school? Beyond that, what of the behavior toward the other species of life, the environment, and the planet?

—-Allan Ward, *Beyond the Visible Spectrum*

Contents

Foreword   ix

Introduction   xiii

Why Small Group Ministry?   1

What to Do Before You Start   13

Choosing, Appointing and Training Facilitators   25

Three Kinds of Covenants   37

Expanding Circles and Welcoming New Friends   47

The Varieties of Small Group Experience   57

A New Model of Ministry   69

Current Issues, Future Directions   79

Principle, Compassion, Openness and Hope   93

Sample Materials   101

Resources   113

Foreword

Small Group Ministry is the hope of our movement. This guide to Small Group Ministry documents, explains, describes, and encourages the small wonders in our lives that make believers of us all. Bob Hill knows that our Unitarian Universalist belief in human dignity is not a creed; it's a liturgical practice. He knows that we are a community of communities, a congregation of congregations, a people who practice right relationship as Small Group Ministry for ourselves, for each other, and for the world. Seeing is believing. This book is about vision.

As Unitarian Universalists, we affirm right relationship as a reverential act. This affirmation is our covenantal act together as a noncreedal people. This is our religious history. Today, we are doing it ten at a time as an embedded ritual practice of our congregational life.

Why does the new form of Small Group Ministry work so well for us today? Why is this ministry transforming our religious movement? Why do so many participants feel new joy and fulfillment and discover new meaning in their lives when they follow the simple, covenantal procedures for practicing right relationship in these small group settings?

Thanks to Bob's book, the answers to these questions are at hand. The techniques, models, references, and suggestions needed to understand, practice, develop, or simply to begin this work are right here. Bob's answers are not doctrinal. They are as concrete as a human heart that is no longer lonely, warm as the place of human embrace that rekindles the sacred ground of our faith.

Bob had to write this book. He could not remain silent because the power of this movement in our midst has transformed him. He's really a covenant group practical evangelist. As a minister, he's got the vision; as a district executive, he attends to the structural issues and concerns; and as a veteran journalist, he records the detail. The transformative power of his work is in its concreteness. Salvation is not theory here. It's meeting time. Community action. Personal commitment. Praxis. It's the place where the stranger is no longer alone.

I discovered the power of Bob Hill's own Small Group Ministry first at his 2000 General Assembly workshop, then as an avid reader of his *Covenant Group Newsletter* and finally through my ongoing work with him to develop the contemporary Unitarian Universalist covenant group movement he has done so much to foster. Like Bob, I have taken the covenant group message on the road and I have seen and felt, firsthand, the power of this new form of spiritual life in our congregations.

A particularly vivid image comes to mind. Several years ago I spent an evening discussing Small Group Ministry with members of a New England church who were interested in starting a covenant group program. At the end of my formal remarks, I asked the members of the audience if they might be willing to simply get together in small groups over a meal and talk about their unmet needs in their church.

One of the most respected elder statesmen of the church stood up and slowly walked to the front of the assembly, faced his fellow congregants and said he was interested in joining a covenant group. He had wanted something like this for years, he said, because he was lonely. "I do not have any friends," he finally confessed. Waves of shock rolled through the gathering. How could *he* be lonely? He was a revered and beloved member of the congregation, a pillar of the church. Many people expressed disbelief.

When the group quieted down, the man spoke again, saying, "Every man in this room who is my age knows what I am talking about. Our social upbringing has taught us not to talk about our feelings. We are not supposed to be emotionally vulnerable or close to anyone except our wives."

As I listened to him, something changed. I could hear his heart beating. I could hear my heart beating. I could hear other hearts beating in the room.

At that moment, we were all one heart and thus all of one breath. One deep, long, loving breath infused each heart with new life. (Let's not forget that the Hebrew word for *spirit* refers to a movement of air, wind, the breath of life itself.)

And at that moment, I learned why covenant groups are transforming our Unitarian Universalist movement today. They are ministries for the heart.

Blessed be.

Thandeka
June 2003

Introduction

Guided by reason and intuition, and drawing on new insights as well as from the wisdom of the past, Unitarian Universalism is a religion uniquely suited to this time of rapidly expanding knowledge and sometimes startling change. Most Unitarian Universalists believe this is true. Many recognize that there are millions of people on this continent and elsewhere who need what we have to offer and that service to such people is our reason for existing. So why are we managing to serve so few? Why is the membership of the Unitarian Universalist Association expanding at the rate of only about one new member per congregation per year?

The short answer is *contentiousness.* The longer answer is that because of our theological diversity, we have not organized our congregations in ways that invite open expression of beliefs and life experiences. Lacking the safety of structures that encourage the sharing of commonality-rich stories, we have attended to our differences, argued among ourselves, and scared away the spiritually needy who come to us in search of what we promise. Not that we should avoid all debate or seek perfect harmony. Any church going through changes will experience conflict. It is something closer to squabbling, however, that has often diverted us from our purpose. Pervasive divisiveness has driven away most of the searchers and seekers who have come through our front doors. Focusing on our disagreements, we ignore our

Sunday morning visitors while we draw one another into the verbal battles that some of us, but few of our guests, find invigorating. Our contentiousness has driven away members as well. In recent years, I have been struck by the lonely resignation of some strong and dedicated Unitarian Universalists who confessed to me that they were leaving their churches in search of religious communities that might be able to attend more deeply and respectfully to their needs for spiritual growth.

So I was ripe for the promise of a way to move beyond divisiveness when Glenn Turner told me about Small Group Ministry. He was calling it *meta-church* in 1997, using the term popularized by Carl George, author of several books for evangelical Christian churches. Glenn had heard the message of small group organization from an interim minister in Portland, Maine, Frances Buckmaster. Turner took her advice, began adapting what he found in George's books and tapes, and spread the message to Calvin Dame and his congregation in Augusta, Maine, and then to me. As excited as explorers on the beach of a never-mapped island, Turner, Dame, and I poured over all the materials we could find on the meta-church techniques of highly successful congregations of other faiths. It took a while for us to learn that we were not the first Unitarian Universalists investigating this territory. In fact, James Robinson had begun using small group organization in Brewster, Massachusetts, in 1982, with great success, and Brent Smith was applying his own adaptations of small group methods in Tulsa, Oklahoma.

Somehow, neither these home-grown breakthroughs nor the megasuccesses of Christian churches using small group approaches had been called to the attention of our ministers or lay leaders. That oversight is being corrected now by a grassroots movement that has come to be identified primarily by one of two generic terms. From George's term *meta-church,* two names for these techniques have evolved among us. One is *Small Group Ministry,* and the other is *Covenant Group Ministry,* and I will use both in this book. Our congregations, of course, have felt free to invent their own titles; they use scores of names, many of which refer to the flaming chalice symbol, including *Chalice Circles* and *Chalice Groups.* Sometimes the names chosen are lighthearted and innovative. The young adult group at First Unitarian Universalist Church in Austin, Texas, for example, called its covenant group for people new to the church *NUUVies,* and when the NUUVies reached maximum size and spun off a new group, that covenant group called itself *Old NUUs.*

The names vary, but any group intending to be a part of Small Group Ministry must adhere closely to the six defining elements and conduct meetings in keeping with the basic elements of a given format. These elements are listed below. Although our churches have always had many other kinds of small groups—often effective and highly valued—this book is about a specific type of group with particular characteristics having to do with size, leadership, and intention. Small Group Ministry provides relational groups designed to build, in the midst of our diverse memberships, centers of trust and friendship that remain closely connected to the church or fellowship within which they exist.

Elements of Small Group Ministry

Size. The ideal covenant group size is eight to ten people. The group should have at least three or four people plus the facilitator and never more than twelve, including the facilitator.

Frequency of meetings. The group should meet at least once a month and may meet twice a month or even weekly in someone's home or at church (if a quiet, private, living room-like setting is regularly available).

Format. The format must combine worshipful and/or centering readings or rituals and personal check-in periods at the start and at the end. (See the recommended format below.)

Facilitators. A facilitator is a woman or man who has been chosen and trained by the minister(s) (or in societies with no minister, by someone chosen by a small steering committee). The minister (or designated leader) then facilitates a covenant group for facilitators so that the training is ongoing and shared.

Empty Chair. Always keep at least one chair empty, to symbolize those not yet reached who need us and to suggest the expectation that a new group will be "born from" this group when membership gets to ten or so.

Covenants. During the second meeting, agree on a behavioral covenant—on how members wish to be with each other. Later, agree on at least one service to perform for the church each year. Twice a year, find a way of doing, as a group, something beneficial in the larger community.

Standard Format

- An opening reading from a Unitarian Universalist source (our hymn book contains enough material to sustain a covenant group for many, many months).
- A check-in period during which each person is asked to briefly state his or her answer to a question such as, What's on your mind today? What do you need to leave behind for a couple of hours in order to be fully present here?
- A time for the focus or purpose of the meeting. The topic or activity can be whatever the group prefers, so long as it is consistent with our Purposes and Principles and the mission of the sponsoring congregation. The focus should be more on sharing than on debating.
- The closing check-out. The facilitator asks each person for a word or phrase that says something about how she or he is feeling as the meeting draws to an end.
- A closing reading. Again, it should be from a standard Unitarian Universalist source.

Writing some months ago for my e-mail newsletter, *Covenant Group News,* a member of our congregation in Tacoma, Washington, Mark Backus, said he'd been looking all his life for the sort of experiences our small groups provide—in high school, in college, in medical school, and in his professional life. When he finally discovered Small Group Ministry, he found the experience transformative:

> My participation has helped me to see the world from many different perspectives, to grow and to change, and to nurture those directions that are most likely to take me closer to that Holy Grail, the "good life." I find myself listening better, caring more about others, thinking more clearly, and spending more time on the process rather than the goal. The most democratic and educational of all our institutions is not the voting booth or the school, but the small group.

"At the grass-roots level," sociologist Robert Wuthnow says in *Sharing the Journey,* "members and leaders of small groups need to be aware that they are part of a massive phenomenon that has the potential to change American society, for good or for ill." The fact that the small group movement has permeated our congregations without support from our elected and appointed folks at headquarters may be a part of its appeal to some of us. The recent shift to active Association support, though, should strengthen what is already as close to being a "massive phenomenon" as we Unitarian Universalists are likely to see, given our size.

No other significant change in how we do things has been met with so much acceptance and so little resistance. The only published opposition to covenant groups that I've seen is in a journal article by a theological school professor who dismisses Small Group Ministry as "irrelevant narcissism" that compares unfavorably with preconsolidation Universalist combativeness. Others who look back with nostalgia to the good old days of no-nonsense, tough-minded intellectual debate may feel that Small Group Ministry is too touchy-feely, intuitive, and conflict averse. We are moving away from the bare-knuckled debate over controversial issues that characterized early Unitarian Universalism, and with good cause. In the 1960s and 1970s, many of us were embroiled in the antiwar movement, while various other controversies involving racism, women's liberation, sexual freedom, and drug use raged around and through our congregations. Our recent membership decline began then and lasted a decade and a half. Many of us took firm and laudable stands based on principle and believe, to this day, that doing so was worth the cost.

We soon may feel compelled again to take similarly difficult stands on potentially divisive issues.

Covenant groups offer us contexts in which to speak to our concerns with the expectation that our views will be heard and respected, safe settings in which there can be consideration of issues without rancor. I have been present when potentially divisive issues were confronted and considered without animosity because they were raised in the context of a covenant group. Members of the group had come to know and trust each other. Differences of opinion and viewpoint that might have drawn disdain or worse in another context were listened to and heard. Such respectful interactions are at the heart of this approach to church organization, and it is my hope that Small Group Ministry can help us deal with such issues more humanely and more effectively throughout our association of Unitarian Universalist congregations.

Have we ever been more in need of a widely accepted, carefully implemented improvement in our ways of "doing church"? Ours is a momentous time of hopefulness and fear. The voice of liberal religion needs to be heard at the White House, in Congress, in our school board meetings, and in our neighborhoods. Fortunately, Unitarian Universalism is moving beyond some of the barriers that have kept us small and inconsequential for a century and a half. Over the last couple of decades we have gradually begun, in practice as well as in proclamations, to honor intuition along with reason as guides to the major religious questions. And now we are beginning to move away from what one observer has referred to as our "recreational argumentation," away from contentiousness and toward community. Small Group Ministry furthers both trends and makes it possible for us to serve more people.

Most of our congregations get plenty of visitors. Those that keep records usually find that the number of people who visit each year equals or exceeds their total membership number. Our problem is that up until now, we have been unable to keep our visitors coming back long enough to discover in Unitarian Universalism a religious home. A well-placed leader of the Church of the Latter-Day Saints who has studied Unitarian Universalism once commented, "Relative to total membership, you Unitarian Universalists draw in a higher proportion of visitors each year than any other religious body. If you ever solve your retention problem, you'll be dangerous."

Covenant groups help us to more effectively welcome individuals who have not yet discovered that we offer the church homes they need. Why do people seek out churches? Many come to our congregations in times of personal crisis, wanting community and a bit of help with getting through the day. They need friends with whom they may recharge their souls. Other visitors come seeking connection to larger meaning and deeper feeling, to a sense of greater significance. They need their lives to matter on this earth. Actually, all of us, members and visitors alike, have these needs. Sometimes we may be focused more on the personal (give us our daily bread) and sometimes more on the global (forgive us our trespasses, or better yet, help us to trespass less against others and against nature), but we bring both kinds of needs to our churches. We are right to look to our Unitarian Universalist churches to help us save the world and get through the day. Small Group Ministry is a way of saying to visitors, "We have anticipated your coming, and we have provided ways for you to meet others in a relaxed setting that encourages conversation." Small Group Ministry gives us a way to make our visitors feel more welcomed and to serve better the thousands of religiously liberal people who need us.

Because we are finally ready and able to fulfill our potential, some of us believe that we may be on the edge of a golden age of Unitarian Universalism. We may soon be more influential in our nation and in our world, able to help avert the worst of what we fear. To speak of saving the world is to invite the disdain of "realists." If there really is hope for our freedoms and for justice, one way of furthering such hope is through a resurgence of Unitarian Universalism founded in Small Group Ministry.

You can be a part of a quiet and effective revolution. The first step is finding and joining with nine or so others who meet regularly with a facilitator and covenant to serve each other, their church, and their larger community.

This book is about that revolution.

Why Small Group Ministry?

Consider the case of the Fellowship Church of Grapevine, Texas. This Baptist church's three thousand-seat sanctuary is usually just about full, and its ministers claim, reasonably enough, that the church serves more than sixteen thousand adults and children every weekend in five worship services—two on Saturday evenings and three on Sunday mornings. The church's membership was about five thousand some years back, seven thousand a year later, and nine thousand the year after that. In July of 2002, their first-ever 8:30 A.M. Sunday service attracted fifteen hundred worshipers.

You may want to review those numbers, because they tell us something shocking. This single Baptist church just north of the Dallas-Fort Worth airport has added more new members over the last four years than we have added to the 1,050 churches and fellowships of the Unitarian Universalist Association combined.

"So what?" you may be saying, "That's not us." You're right, but Fellowship Church is not a typical Baptist church, either. No doubt this church is appealing to mainstream, religiously conservative folks, identified as "traditionals" and "moderns" by sociologist Paul H. Ray in his 1996 study of the lifestyles, values, and worldviews of Americans. This category makes up about 75 percent of the population and Unitarian Universalist churches hold little appeal for them. Still, we haven't done nearly so well, proportionally, with the remaining 25 percent who are more like us.

Being Baptist is not what made Fellowship Church huge. Lots of nearby churches preach middle-of-the-road-to-conservative Christian theology and have not boomed. One-third of Baptist General Conference congregations, according to Lyle Schaller, average seventy-three members or fewer at worship on Sundays. Outstanding preaching does not seem to be the cause of Fellowship Church's growth either. A casually dressed minister, preaching from a few notes and a Bible, can offer a sermon in which he contrasts the uncertainties of modern life with the certainties of a "Christ-reliant" life, and he can do so calmly, with no special oratorical flourishes or earth-shaking insights, and only passable humor. And his church continues to boom. Slick production techniques combined with the latest video and music enhancements may have some effect, but the church met for a time in a school and members spent twenty-three hours every weekend trucking chairs, tables, and other gear in and out. The technological enhancement of their services must have been less slick then. Still, the church grew. Why?

From the beginning, Fellowship Church has been organized around small groups it calls HomeTeams. On the Sunday of my first visit there, in the expansive, two-floor gathering area into which the worshipers file after the service, there are signs everywhere to let people know what the church offers: small groups for singles, married couples, and families focusing on various interests and activities. A recent order of service had this message:

> Looking for new friendships? Joining a HomeTeam is your next step! HomeTeams are small groups of married and single adults who meet in homes across the Metroplex for Bible study and fellowship. Stop by the Guest Services Kiosk in the Atrium for more information. Pick up a list of HomeTeams in your area and get involved!

How small are these groups? Each of the married-couple HomeTeams consists of four or five couples; and the church has about 120 of them, plus about an equal number of HomeTeams for singles.

Our members need what Small Group Ministry offers just as much as members of other churches do. At a UUA General Assembly several years ago, two ministers told of deathbed statements they'd heard from the lips of parishioners. In one case, a woman complained that she had been a "poor Unitarian Universalist" because what she had wanted from her church was the opportunity to talk with others about what mattered most to her, and she had never made that happen. The other story concerned a man who complained about church experience by telling his minister, "All I ever wanted was the chance to talk with others about life's journey." If their churches had known about and implemented Small Group Ministries, these two Unitarian Universalists might have had less regret at the ends of their lives.

Small Group Ministry techniques are rooted deeply in the past, including our own heritage. The success of Fellowship Church and others like it results from the use of an approach to ministry that seems new to us but is at least a couple of thousand years old. The evangelical Christian ministers who write about meta-church issues find in the New Testament indications that early Christians met in small groups in homes for fellowship, study, and discipleship long before the word *church* carried any connotations of "building." A flyer from another Baptist church using HomeTeams notes that "small group meetings in homes were the foundation of the early church. Acts 5:42 tells us that the people met 'in temple courts' (large group worship) and 'from house to house' (small group fellowship)." Some argue that Christianity, after its infancy in small groups, lost a source of vitality in the third century, when Christians began to put up church buildings.

Our own history offers the example of Universalist George de Benneville, who had a "house church" in the mid-1700s near Reading, Pennsylvania. John Morgan says there were Universalist groups in Rhode Island and the mid-Atlantic states that met in small study circles once a week to share their stories, discuss the Sunday sermon, and interpret scripture. What these Universalists in the early days of our country seemed to have understood is something that many of us are learning all over again—something Morgan heard Dr. James Luther Adams say in a lecture at Andover Newton Theological School a quarter of a century ago: People come to churches for "ultimacy and intimacy." In a February, 2000 issue of *Covenant Group News,* Morgan writes,

> I have found Adams' theory to meet the test of parish ministry. People come into our communities looking for a place to belong (intimacy) and a place to seek meaning (ultimacy) about living and dying and the spaces between. And though I hoped the churches I served could meet these two needs, I sometimes found how short we fell.

Thus Small Group Ministry serves people better than our standard ways of operating our churches. Our people need the inspiration and intimacy it provides. And this new-to-us way of serving has roots deep in history and our own heritage.

There are at least four additional reasons or facts, though, that explain why Small Group Ministry has spread so quickly and broadly across our Association. These four auspicious facts not only help explain the early success of what Mark Backus called "the most democratic and educational of all our institutions" but also offer us reason for hope for continued deepening and widening of our faith.

Going with the Flow

The first auspicious fact underlying Small Group Ministry's success is that our small group movement is part of the larger, nationwide trend documented in Robert Wuthnow's studies of small groups in our country. The last time we were able to bring about radical change in how we did things was when we were working for the equality of women in the 1960s and 1970s. We made significant changes within our churches and our Association in those years, and we felt successful in our attempts to influence others to move in the same directions. Perhaps our efforts were buoyed more than we recognized by the flow of change around us, in the larger culture. Conversely, perhaps our less-successful antiracism efforts have been hampered (or at least not aided) by the racism of a culture in which civil rights gains are being eroded and racism continues to be a tragically offensive reality. Appreciation of the benefits of small group organization in our churches, like our past recognition of the need for changes in how women were being treated, rides on the crest of a larger cultural trend.

Community and Spirituality

According to Wuthnow, the millions of Americans engaged in the "deeply populist" small group movement in the larger culture are moving away from some traditional values. One might guess otherwise, because nearly two-thirds of all small groups Wuthnow studied are connected to churches or synagogues, and many of the Christian megachurches using small group methods are at least somewhat connected to fundamentalist denominations. Nevertheless, Wuthnow says, people drawn to the small group movement tend to be fed up with large-scale institutions in general and reject "the received wisdom embodied in formal creeds, doctrines, and ideologies."

Wuthnow argues that the small group movement is altering American society "by changing our understandings of community and by redefining spirituality. . . . The quest for spirituality . . . has animated much of the small group movement." We

Unitarian Universalists have become less and less bound to the limits of reason and empiricism. We have become—in keeping with what we've always said we believed about respecting each person's quest for truth in regard to the major issues of mortal life—more and more tolerant of the language of the heart and spirit, up to and including the *nonrational,* a term that these days we are less likely to read as being synonymous with *irrational.* The small group movement, both in our churches and in the nation, seems to be furthering greater openness to spiritual exploration.

Dealing with Diversity

The techniques of Small Group Ministry offer us ways to overcome one of our greatest challenges: finding unity in the context of our diversity. "Diversity," Wuthnow says, "is clearly one of the reasons why the small-group movement has been so successful." He also notes, "Spirituality within small groups . . . is extraordinarily diverse." Because our greatest diversity in Unitarian Universalism is in how we understand the world theologically and philosophically, we have an inherent need for situations in which our deepest beliefs do not become divisive. Our churches are more interesting when they accommodate variety, but our Unitarian Universalist diversity has often been a source of division rather than strength. As we struggled with race issues in the late 1960s and early 1970s, for example, or when many of us, but not all, opposed the war in Vietnam, the fabric of our Association was weakened.

We have sought to deal with diversity through debate, public forums, and *Robert's Rules of Order.* We have taken a strength—our willingness to question and to apply reason to religious claims and dogmas—and made of it a fetish. Some of our smaller congregations (fewer all the time, fortunately) make "talk-back," a time just after each sermon in which congregants may comment upon what they've just heard, a part of their every-Sunday ritual. Others have preservice forums devoted to verbal battle, often pitting a dozen or so devotees of debate against one another, week after week. Defended in the name of intellectual rigor but labeled *recreational argumentation* by Dr. Allan Ward, a covenant group facilitator at the Unitarian Universalist Church of Little Rock, Arkansas, these exchanges serve their participants. To individuals who do not find arguing recreational, however, these forums can be disconcertingly contentious.

Covenant groups encourage listening more than speech making, discussion more than debate, and the sharing of personal stories more than critique. Hearing one another's stories over time, people become more accepting. Like Backus, they find themselves listening better and caring more. Trust begins to grow. In covenant groups, representatives of various points of view have the chance to hear and understand each other.

For most of us there is only one Unitarian Universalist church within driving distance. In only a few urban centers do we offer a choice of "flavors." The various kinds of small groups serve churches, Wuthnow says, as different models of cars serve the automobile industry, which "would have folded shop long ago had it continued to make only the family sedan." Covenant groups in our churches allow those with Buddhist, humanist, Unitarian Universalist Christian, and other perspectives to experience and express their beliefs in religious contexts that supplement the corporate worship of Sunday mornings. By offering greater satisfaction to more members with radically different religious outlooks through covenant groups in which their views may be heard respectfully, we can pull back from divisiveness and reveal the strengths that our theological differences do, in fact, bring us.

Millions Who Need Us

Another auspicious fact is the existence of several million people in this country who share many of our values and attitudes and consider themselves to be alone in the world because they don't see themselves reflected in the media. They are the "isolated many" identified by sociologist Paul H. Ray. Drawing on focus groups, interviews, and surveys of about 100,000 Americans, Ray finds that about a quarter of our population is made up of people who are idealistic, altruistic, and religiously more liberal than other Americans. He calls them the *Cultural Creatives*.

Ray first published his study (sponsored by the Institute for Noetic Sciences and the Fetzer Institute) in 1996; he and his wife, Sherry Ruth Anderson, published a book in 2000 following up on that study: *The Cultural Creatives: How 50 Million People Are Changing the World.* Ray studied people's changing values and lifestyles, and he found that there are three major cultures in America today. The *Traditionals,* who make up about 29 percent of the U.S. adult population, include conservatives and the religious right. Not quite half the U.S. population, 47 percent, Ray labels as the *Moderns.* These people have an essentially materialistic/hedonistic orientation, their highest priorities being personal success, consumerism, materialism, and technological development.

And then there is the fastest-growing cultural group in the United States, the *Cultural Creatives,* who have many characteristics familiar to Unitarian Universalists:

- They have a direct connection to the movements of the 1960s, and they share these distinctive values: ecological sustainability, globalism, women's issues, altruism, self-actualization, spirituality, social conscience, optimism, integrity, authenticity, holism, and direct personal experience.
- Cultural Creatives are the readers of the world, watching less than half as much television as their cultural counterparts, and they have a much higher education level than the Traditionals or the Moderns.
- As of Ray's 1995 study, the Cultural Creatives had a relatively high average income: $47,000 per year. Six out of ten are women. And their median age is forty-two—well below the Unitarian Universalist median age of fifty-five or so. Cultural Creatives are evenly distributed through the country, and their racial profile parallels that of the general population.

Being "information junkies," they scan the world and make their own syntheses. They are not very impressed with authority. They are thinking intuitives. "On the deepest level," Ray writes, Cultural Creatives "are powerfully attuned to global issues and whole systems. Their icon is a photograph taken by an astronaut that shows the earth as a blue pearl hanging in black space."

Many Unitarian Universalists, perhaps most, will recognize themselves as Cultural Creatives or at least as their compatriots. Ray and Anderson note that the roots of Cultural Creative beliefs and attitudes stretch back through what they call "consciousness movements," to Europe and to the American Transcendentalists, including Ralph Waldo Emerson, Margaret Fuller, and Henry David Thoreau. Ray and Anderson believe the Cultural Creatives are leading our nation in a "cultural awakening" and that they are deeply involved in "a great heterogeneous mélange of movements, organizations, and trends" with a common intention to "throw open the windows and doors of the musty old mind-sets we live in, shake the dust out of the covers we wrap around our bodies, and in a thousand old and new ways, guide whoever is willing to show up and pay attention to a fresh experience of being human."

A great many Cultural Creatives, including the individuals that Ray calls *"Core Cultural Creatives,"* are at least nominally members of conventional churches. More of them than of the general population, though, identify themselves as secular, and even those who are in churches "are conducting their search for the sacred along innovative lines," "tend toward theological liberalism," and "make their own synthesis from several traditions." They have a strong interest in self-actualization and see nature as sacred. "As Core Cultural Creatives bring consciousness into their daily lives," Ray and Anderson observe, "they inevitably address our larger culture's lack of support for inner work and spiritual concerns."

This brings us back, of course, to Small Group Ministries, our new/old way of providing support for inner work and the addressing of spiritual concerns. We Unitarian Universalists often complain about, or boast of, our isolation in the larger culture. So do Cultural Creatives, because, Ray says, "their views are rarely represented in the mainstream media, which is mostly owned and operated according to the Modern world view. . . . Little of what they read gives them any evidence of their huge numbers." Speaking as a Cultural Creative himself, Ray says, "We don't have enough connections with each other. We need communities that work."

Our covenant groups are communities that work. Shouldn't a religion of tolerance, compassion, openness, and hope—a religion guided by reason, intuition, and principle—be tailor-made for Cultural Creatives? We've drawn thousands of them through our front doors in recent decades. Some of them stuck. But the vast majority did not. If they had, our continental growth rate would have averaged more than, not less than, 1 percent per year. We didn't know how to welcome them, help them make connections, and encourage their spiritual explorations in safe settings. Now we do.

Wanting a Friend

Allan Ward, the covenant group facilitator at our Little Rock congregation is professor emeritus of speech communication at the University of Arkansas. He has asked his students, year after year, "What do you personally want most in your own communication?" The most frequent answer from persons of all ages and backgrounds is "to find other human beings to talk with without barriers or reservations." Students say they want a community in which they can be "totally and openly themselves," Ward reported in a recent sermon, adding that "the majority say they do not have even one such person, but they are seeking such a community." A police officer told one of Ward's classes that gang members and churchgoers have something in common: Both groups want and need community, and members of these otherwise diverse groups offer virtually identical lists when asked their reasons for joining.

When Ward asked one communications class what sort of religious community they desired, they said they wanted a community with the following characteristics:

- Members of the community like each other.
- Members trust each other.
- Members can talk about everything without arguing, taking unchangeable positions, or trying to convince or dominate.
- The community can look at the cosmic aspects of existence and at the same time deal with the hourly details.
- The community explores the accumulated experimentation of human beings over millennia to glean the best aspects.
- The community is a supportive group that considers the various forms of reverence, learning, and self-insightfulness without drawing conclusions, but rather continuing to make discoveries.
- Members of the community share certain common skills: the ability to describe ideas and feelings clearly, share intuitive flashes without having to defend them, and appreciate the safety of rational thought that weighs evidence and evaluates its sources.
- The community is made up of every possible kind of diversity—all ethnicities and traditions—but has the ability to work together, appreciating differences in people rather than feeling threatened.
- The community provides a place where children grow up with an extended family of explorers who respect them and discuss a range of life experiences with them.

As this list was being generated, one person in the classroom was quiet. Challenged by a more talkative student to say where such a group might be found, she came out of deep concentration to say that such a group exists. "It's the Unitarian Universalists," she said. With perhaps more experience of Unitarian Universalism, Ward notes that this woman's remark called to mind Rev. Martin Luther King Jr.'s saying that our nation's guarantee of freedom and democracy is a promissory note, a potential that we can all help to become a reality. As a covenant group facilitator, though, Ward could affirm, "We are in that process now."

Deeper as Well as Wider

Some say we Unitarian Universalists shouldn't be "trying to grow for growth's sake." Granted. If we want to promote the values we claim to find important, however, we need to stop being statistically insignificant. When the *Wall Street Journal* ran a front-page story about the test scores of high school graduates, the headline said students identifying themselves as Reformed Jews ranked highest. The accompanying chart showed that the scores of Unitarian Universalist students, in fact, topped the list. One can only surmise that we were too few to matter to the headline writers.

Similarly, after our General Assembly's passage of a resolution calling for change in our nation's destructive policy known as the War on Drugs, a critic sympathetic to our resolution's views immediately thought of the 1959 Peter Sellers movie *The Mouse that Roared,* a satirical comedy in which a tiny country declares war on the United States and sends its only ship, under full sail, to New York to be defeated and become eligible for foreign aid. Small is not always beautiful. In the give and take of political and social debate in today's world, small is often irrelevant.

Small Group Ministry, in contrast, can bring enough difference to our churches to change our Association's story. It gives us a way to better serve one another and all those others who need us. When Small Group Ministry changes the culture of a church, that church becomes less contentious and more open hearted. A subscriber to *Covenant Group News* recently wrote about a single covenant group that produced enough change to avoid what could have been a serious rift in her laity-led fellowship.

The lone covenant group had been meeting for less than a year when all heck broke loose one Sunday over a perceived instance of intolerance toward Unitarian Universalist Christians. One element of the controversy concerned a member's behavior while he was, some members believed, under the influence of alcohol. The fight that was developing was the kind that can drive away members and then, like a never-quite-extinguished forest fire, linger in a small group for years. In this instance, though, the fight was over in two weeks. The woman, who asked to remain anonymous, said people "talked out their differences and came to new understandings of each other." How was this crisis resolved so uncharacteristically well? She concluded,

> Many of the covenant group members were involved, directly or indirectly, with this controversy. We used the openness, mutual respect and support we'd found within the group to embolden us to model a different way of behaving for the whole church. I do credit the covenant group model and our use of it with providing the support, the courage, and the way to move our church through what could have been a very divisive time.

In Numbers and in Love

The rapidly growing Thoreau Congregation in Stafford, Texas, calls its Small Group Ministries *Friendship Circles*. The facilitator of one, Mary Fitzgerald, wrote an assessment of their program that suggests why Small Group Ministry, done thoroughly and well, can carry us deeper and wider: "Our Friendship Circles have been a wonderful venue for new and old members to connect. We talk about our lives and deepen the connection to each other as people. I truly believe covenant groups are the way to grow a church, in numbers and in love and connectedness."

Recalling his doubts when he first heard about meta-church groups from Glenn Turner, Calvin Dame said, "I was skeptical of the idea that people would commit to more meetings in their lives. It seemed to me that getting people out to committee meetings and church functions was already like pulling teeth, so I could not imagine that anyone would make an open ended commitment to come out twice a month for anything." Events in the Augusta church Dame serves changed his views. In his Small Group Ministry handbook he wrote, "I was wrong because I seriously underestimated the hunger in our hearts for real community and for spiritual challenge and growth." When fully adopted by our congregations and undertaken thoroughly, Small Group Ministry allows us to serve well the basic needs of our own members and many others who need liberal religion.

Should Unitarian Universalists have buildings that seat three thousand? Should we seek to build churches that serve more than sixteen thousand every weekend? Probably not. Our appeal is to a smaller portion of the population of our regions than the segments to which Baptists and others appeal.

So far Unitarian Universalist large churches have seemed to hit a "glass ceiling" at about 1,500 members, with only two or three breaking through for brief periods, according to the UUA's staff person assigned to our "large churches," Stefan Jonasson. He believes that "four-digit churches" need two aspects ours have lacked: suitable governance structures and "sustained, meaningful programs in Small Group Ministry." Whatever our maximum church size may turn out to be it is important for us to note that the number of people in the United States, Canada, and elsewhere who need liberal religious community is surely a hundred times larger than the number we have reached thus far. Our path will be different from the paths of other religious organizations, but this much is clear: The possibilities that Small Group Ministry opens to us are, for all practical purposes, unlimited.

What To Do Before You Start

A first step for many congregations thinking about starting Small Group Ministry may be clarification of purpose. Drawing upon the "enormous literature" on small groups in our larger culture, Wuthnow says a small group's sponsoring organization needs a "well thought-out, explicitly formulated statement of purpose." Does your church or fellowship have a clearly stated plan for serving those who need Unitarian Universalism? Jerry King, UUA capital campaign consultant, says,

> I think it would be helpful if, before beginning Small Group Ministry, the congregations would review the basic reasons they are in existence. Some work by the congregation on their mission, while probably not absolutely necessary, would enhance the process and could increase a congregation's feeling of accomplishment as they see the results of their Small Group Ministries.

In *Small Groups in the Church,* Alban Institute author Thomas Kirkpatrick agrees, saying, "The process of developing and adopting a purpose, goals, and a strategy is vitally important." He urges the widest possible participation in shaping a plan to be presented to the congregation.

Failure to make the strong connection between covenant groups and the congregation's central purpose can result in "thinking too small," and that, Dame believes, is the main source of covenant group failure. Dame said recently,

> This is not just another adult education program, but a very real challenge to Unitarian Universalists to take their faith journeys and our religious communities seriously, and that means struggling with questions of vision, ministry, authority, spiritual growth and service. I don't want people to think that my Augusta church has solved all these problems, but we are a better congregation for having wrestled with them and for embracing the change that has come with Small Group Ministry.

"What's intended is making Small Group Ministry a focus for the entire church with an outreach program and a vision to help extend the ministry of the congregation," Turner has said, adding, "Developing one or two small groups and letting it go at that is not Small Group Ministry." While the addition of even a single covenant group to a church's program expands that congregation's openness to the world and service to its members, a positive change in the church's culture as a result is unlikely.

Wuthnow outlines an approach to creating small groups that may also be useful for Unitarian Universalist groups. First, Wuthnow says, there should be a research and planning phase, during which information can be gathered and adapted to the group's (in our case, the church's) situation, its vision of itself, and its purpose in the community in which it exists. Once that phase is complete, Wuthnow suggests, the next step is selecting leaders and training them. Then, he advises, have a pilot-program phase to allow the group to test its model of organization and to work out unforeseen difficulties.

Small Group Ministry Success Stories

Michael McGee, when he was minister of West Shore Church in Cleveland, began a Small Group Ministry program by using members of his board of trustees as a pilot group. He offered to give board members a chance to learn firsthand what covenant groups are by being facilitator of a group for them for a few months. Enough board members took him up on his offer to allow the pilot project to go forward. As a result, a cadre of excited board members took leadership roles in seeing that a covenant group program was implemented at West Shore Church.

When First Parish in Brewster, Massachusetts, Jim Robinson's congregation, was moving to the midsize or program level, he and his lay leaders surveyed members' interests and then sought facilitators for groups to match those interests. Having begun small group organization in 1982, the congregation had grown to the point of needing two services on Sundays. They had also determined that they wanted their congregation to become more diverse. What all these changes meant, they decided, was that they needed to add ten or twenty new small groups. Robinson recalled during a recent meeting of Small Group Ministry leaders, "What we began with was a study of our members' interests. Using that, we suggested forty possible small groups and let people indicate which ones they might want to join. Then we asked ourselves, 'Who could be a natural leader for that group?' Then we contacted that person." This, of course, was what eventually led to the church's needing to go to three services.

Robinson and his folks have become especially adept at the use of questions. While many of our congregations have put more energy into self-promotion than into learning about their visitors, Robinson's Brewster church routinely asks visitors these days two questions:

- What would this congregation need to be like for you to want to be a part of it?
- What sort of a covenant group would you be interested in joining?

The Unitarian Universalist Community Church of Augusta, Maine and its minister, Dame, followed a path of preparation containing many of the elements Wuthnow outlines. Their guide entitled *A Small Group Ministry Resource Book* offers highlights of their approach. After being persuaded by Turner that they should explore meta-church possibilities, Augusta leaders created an ad hoc committee that met twice a week for six months. Committee members read Carl George's books and reported back to the group. They watched portions of George's videotapes. And they sought out information from other Unitarian Universalist congregations, including Robinson's church and All Souls in Tulsa, Oklahoma. Their choice of the term *Small Group Ministry* grew out of decisions made earlier about the purpose of their church. Dame says in his *Small Group Ministry Resource Book,*

> From the beginning, we envisioned our groups as a way that we could better care for one another. People would be connected at a deeper level than is possible Sunday during the Fellowship Hour, and there would be the

opportunity to pursue some of the deeper spiritual questions which in our lives we so rarely take time for. But these groups would also form the framework in which we could reach out to one another in caring and support, where we could be present in each other's lives in the forms that describe ministry.

Our Augusta church's leaders were clear on their purpose, and they began with research.

Their next step was devising and implementing a strategy for informing and gaining the support of the congregation as a whole. With the research phase completed, members of the ad hoc committee began making sure that information about Small Group Ministry planning was widely disseminated within the congregation. They put articles and columns by the minister and the church president in the newsletter, at least one in each issue. There were announcements at Sunday services, and Dame preached on the reasons for what they were doing. Even though the president of the church and two members of the board were a part of the ad hoc committee, the committee was careful to report regularly to the board, which eventually received the committee's final proposal. The board endorsed the plan and reported its action to the congregation. Dame says, "We took this part of our planning effort seriously because we believed that we were exploring a program which offered a different paradigm of congregational life, and which held out the prospect of transforming our church. If it were to be successful, we would need to bring as many people as we could along with us."

They were successful. "Continuous curiosity and conversation" accompanied the ad hoc committee's announcements and newsletter articles, and the congregation was prepared by the time the program was launched. After four years of Small Group Ministry, our Augusta church had about half its membership participating in its more than a dozen groups, many of which had met continuously since the beginning. A couple of the original groups ceased to exist, but there is usually at least one group in the process of formation. A steering committee works with the minister to consider problems, look ahead, and plan and the church has added a part-time Small Group Ministry coordinator to its staff.

Although preparing properly for Small Group Ministry often requires lots of time, a motivated, experienced minister meeting a congregation with an eagerness to proceed can sometimes move more quickly than normal. Arthur Vaeni was called to our Olympia Unitarian Universalist Congregation in Washington in August 2001. He had small group organization experience in his previous congregation,

Starr King Unitarian Universalist Fellowship of Plymouth, New Hampshire. Vaeni had planned to introduce the Olympia congregation to Small Group Ministry ideas during his first year and to begin the program at the start of his second year with the church. Fortunately or otherwise, three members of the congregation attended a district-sponsored workshop on Small Group Ministry and returned full of enthusiasm. Vaeni recalls,

> In December those three workshop participants along with three members of the Committee on Ministry crafted a plan for starting the groups in April. I thought we were pushing it to try to do things that quickly, but we agreed that if we were to introduce [the program] in the spring, it had to be early enough so the groups could begin to coalesce before the inevitable disruptions of summer. We also agreed that if it didn't feel as though it was coming together as spring approached, then we would postpone until this fall.

Vaeni and these six people, working as a start-up committee, had to meet often to pull off the program's beginning in such a short time. They put articles and columns in the church newsletter to let folks know what they were doing and thinking. They produced a brochure. They held question-and-answer sessions after church services. They presented a Small Group Ministry skit during the announcement periods of Sunday services. They recruited and trained facilitators. And, on the day set aside for sign-ups, Vaeni led a service focused on Small Group Ministry. The result? Within a year the church had eleven groups serving about one hundred people.

Beginning in 1997, as new ministers in our extension congregation in Boiling Springs, Pennsylvania, Judy Wells and Duane Fickeisen followed a suggestion from Margaret Beard in the UUA Extension Department and asked their membership committee to organize a series of getting-to-know-you evenings at the homes of members, about fifty widely dispersed folks, who named their church "Unitarian Universalists of Cumberland Valley." With the help of the church's membership committee, gatherings of five or more members were set up. Wells and Fickeisen brought three questions to each gathering. First, people were asked to spend five to ten minutes recounting the highlights of their lives. "Many told us they had never been asked to talk about their lives in this way with people attending to their stories as though they really mattered," Wells and Fickeisen said in an April, 2000 issue of *Covenant Group News.* A second question presented to those gathered in homes was, What has your attention and energy now? What are you excited about, concerned about, dreading, pondering, celebrating? A third question was, How do you anticipate/hope/expect that your relationship with this congregation will affect your life?

By the end of the process, Wells and Fickeisen report, "We had a bunch of little cohorts who had heard each other's life stories and begun to know each other in some depth." Members asked for more such meetings, and the ministers obliged. This time, they focused on questions such as the following: How can we nurture your core, the center of your spirit? How can our faith community help you develop a deeper grounding and resilience that enhances the quality and meaning of your life? A frequent answer was, "More of this!" According to Welles and Fickeisen,

> People appreciated the opportunity to gather in small groups and talk about what really mattered to them, and it was clear that they were hungry for more. Our adult membership has more than doubled and we continue to bring in new members at a steady rate. We have a healthy infrastructure of committees and working groups, and, by our third year, we had accomplished many of the "nuts and bolts" tasks that we thought would take five years or more.

The experience of offering these two levels of getting-to-know-you sessions suggested to them that their new congregation was ripe for covenant groups. Borrowing a term from Hollywood, they think of those sessions as "prequels" to Small Group Ministry.

Leaders of the First Unitarian Universalist Church in Houston, Texas, spent several months learning about the various ways of doing covenant groups in churches before launching their program. They invited their district executive to meet with and "evangelize" the board of the church and then continued their research work, quietly moving toward the launch of the Small Group Ministries they decided to call *Chalice Circles*.

Asked by her board to give part of her time to covenant group work, Gail Lindsay Marriner chose and trained facilitators and cofacilitators for nine Chalice Circles. In January 2001, people were invited to sign up for one of these inital groups if they were willing to commit to attend at least twelve monthly or biweekly meetings. Other Circles were suggested by members, and some of them have been put into place. By the summer, fourteen groups were serving ninety-five members.

One lesson learned, according to Brenda Mendiola, a former president of the church and an early advocate of small group organization, is this: "Keep to the format and the six necessary components." A Circle that abandoned the practice of starting with readings and a check-in and ending with a reading and a check-out, for example, ceased to meet after only a few weeks.

As a Chalice Circle facilitator, Mendiola is part of the First Chalice Group, the covenant group led by Marriner for facilitators and cofacilitators. Mendiola says in reply to a *Covenant Group News* survey question,

> At First Chalice sessions, we address any "burning questions" the facilitators may have and we discuss and/or brainstorm topics such as our "1-Page Manual on Chalice Circles," why we do check-ins and check-outs, what to look for in a co-facilitator and how to select one for recommendation to the ministers, and the development of our own covenant. During the second year of First Chalice meetings, we have started going deeper by sharing our personal stories around central themes.

"Chalice Circles," Mendiola says, "have become one of my passions, and I am so excited that our members have taken the time and effort to put all this in place and to participate." It was while serving as chair of the congregation's nominating committee in 2001 that Mendiola found empirical evidence of the degree to which this program had become a part of how key leaders perceived their church. Mendiola has said,

> The committee interviewed seven church members as potential candidates for four Board positions. When asked what they believed to be critically important "happenings" at First Church, every one of the seven said "Chalice Circles," along with other things like "Children's Religious Education" and "Social Justice activities." I would say that's an indication of early success!

It is also an indication that careful planning can lead to a covenant group program that is deeply imbedded in the church's life, not just a passing fad. Successful Small Group Ministries usually are found in congregations that have relative clarity of purpose, where leaders took time to research and understand small group organization techniques, where there was a thorough process of informing and educating others, where facilitators were carefully chosen and trained, and where leaders were enthusiastic about Small Group Ministry.

What Small Group Ministry Is

One of the biggest dangers the covenant group movement faces is the possibility that a year or a few years from now, congregations will adopt a been-there-done-that-and-failed attitude about Small Group Ministry, when in fact they have tried something less than the full program. The necessary, defining characteristics of Small Group Ministry are in the six fundamental elements and agenda described at the beginning of this book. By omitting a key element or two, by not committing to service beyond the group itself, or by refusing to welcome new members and to birth new groups when membership reaches ten, a Small Group Ministry can fall short of its potential. Failure to attain potential, Alfred North Whitehead says, is sin. The best way to prevent this sin, then, is to understand thoroughly what is involved in Small Group Ministry, to communicate that knowledge broadly, and then to implement carefully, perhaps with a pilot program as a beginning.

McGee, after launching covenant groups in Cleveland, joined a co-ministry in our thousand-member Unitarian Universalist Church of Arlington, Virginia. Starting with six groups in January 2000, he and Joan Gelbein were surprised by the enthusiasm lay leaders brought to the beginnings of covenant groups there. McGee said in a discussion with other Small Group Ministry leaders,

> Covenant groups have brought about a sea-change in the culture of our congregation, or are in the process of doing so. We're teaching people that the culture of our church is to listen to each other, to respect each other, to be honest with each other. This program is having a real impact. It's the open door that lets people find a place where they can really feel at home. If we don't have Covenant Group Ministry, people just turn around and go away.

What Small Group Ministry Is Not

Often, people hearing for the first time about the covenant group movement in our churches say something like, "Oh, we're already doing that. We have lots of small groups." It takes a while for folks to understand that Small Group Ministries are radically different from the other small groups of our congregations.

Our churches have groups that serve a few or a lot of people, and some of them do so quite well. Judith Smith-Valley described a fairly typical array of small groups that were a part of her former First Parish congregation in Kennebunk, Maine, before she and that church began a Small Group Ministry program. The First

Parish congregation had two men's groups, a women's spirituality group, an adult discussion group, and the choir. "New members of the church, the ones who stayed, became active in the church because they got involved in one of these groups," Smith-Valley observes in her doctoral thesis. At least to an acceptable degree, the people in these groups were getting their needs met. As Turner has said, "For many, such programs were entry-points into our churches. They turned them on, gave them what they wanted." Those of us who were once visitors and who have stayed must have found a way into the community. But, Turner writes in an early paper on meta-church techniques, "Only a fraction of our people are involved with such groups. In the small church it's a minute percentage. For most, our churches provide a diet of worship once a week, potluck dinners every few weeks, and a Unitarian Universalist orientation class once in each lifetime."

The two men's groups at First Parish, Kennebunk, were not open to new members. Cakes for the Queen of Heaven groups (women-only gatherings that grew out of a UUA adult education curriculum) in our churches have sometimes declared themselves closed. For a newcomer, finding out about groups, even those that are willing to take in new members, can be difficult. What about those who attended First Parish for a while but did not get involved in any one of that church's groups? "They would drift away or disappear," Smith-Valley said, adding, "It's not easy to move into an established congregation."

Would it have been wise for some of the existing small groups of the Kennebunk church to have tried to become covenant groups? Probably not. Existing groups have their own rules and leadership patterns, even when the members are not well aware of them. Trying to impose on existing groups the radical modifications that would be required to have them become covenant groups is not likely to succeed. Effective small groups that are already in place and serving well should be encouraged in their successful ways. Covenant groups, different from other small groups in the ways we've stated, are intended to serve visitors, new members, and long-time members who are not being adequately served by the church organizations we usually think of when we hear the term *small groups*.

Avoid the Genesis Mistake

In beginning Small Group Ministry in a church, the enthusiasm of leaders—especially the enthusiasm of ministers—is absolutely necessary, but it should not stimulate too-early pronouncements of revolutionary change. Good planning and organizational work should precede any attempt to spread the enthusiasm to the rest of the congregation. In an on-line article warning against "common false starts," one Christian minister urged his colleagues to avoid what he called "the Genesis mistake"—trying to talk the program into existence. A powerful Small Group Ministry sermon accompanied by newsletter articles, but without planning and organization, can backfire even though the first book of the Old Testament says the world itself was spoken into being: "And God said . . . and it was so."

George also warns against starting meta-church work with a big splash in advance of thorough preparation. Perhaps we Unitarian Universalists have a special need to be warned against trying to talk Small Group Ministries into being. We need to find approaches somewhere between the method attributed to God in Genesis, however, and another small group introduction process recommended in evangelical Christian literature that could take between five and seven years. Fortunately, there is middle ground: some months of preparation, probably, but not years.

The Paradox of Formality

For some groups, getting past an allergy to formality and seeing beyond a mythic belief in family-like closeness will be prerequisite to Small Group Ministry. Churches, as they get larger, have to move toward more formal organization to function well. Resistance to increased formality is common all along the path from small to large church sizes, but it is particularly strong in some of our smaller, we're-like-a-family congregations. Members of some of these congregations may resist even the minimal degree of organization required for the planning and implementation of Small Group Ministry.

Recent studies indicate that congregations perceived by their members to be "like a family" are among our slowest-growing congregations. Members of our fastest-growing congregations are much less likely to choose that phrase to describe their churches. So, our groups most intent on maintaining the informal, family-feeling aspects of their congregations are the least likely to provide programs that welcome and draw in new folks eager for, among other things, close community.

Leaders of "family" fellowships or churches sometimes wonder why so few of their visitors stick around to become members of their relaxed, informal congregations and why their guests move on to join instead the stuffy, formal churches down the road. Here's a hint: Joining most families involves either an accident of birth or a long and difficult courtship. Families are not usually inclusive, democratic organizations. Families have implicit, unspoken rules and structures that are not readily obvious to individuals who are not already members. The more formal structure of Small Group Ministry, by contrast, offers explicit rules available to everyone, newcomer and longtimer alike. Explicit rules, being accessible to all, are inclusive and democratic.

If they stayed long enough, might more visitors to our family-style groups learn the implicit rules of membership and become insiders? Perhaps. Most of us who are Unitarian Universalists today probably toughed out an initiation period of hanging around on the edge of a Unitarian Universalist group somewhere. One man said to his wife as they were driving away from a first-time visit to one of our fellowships, "I'm not going to let them treat us like that; we're going back next Sunday!" Shut out of the group's closeness during that first visit and feeling angry, he returned and eventually became president of the fellowship. Few visitors, though, will stay around long enough to ferret out the not-stated rules of inclusion and find ways to break through the walls of a casual, "like-a-family" fellowship or church.

Most of our slow-growing Unitarian Universalist churches and fellowships need organizational change if they are to become able to welcome and integrate those who come to us in search of a liberal-religious home. The need for formal organization is a precondition of attaining closeness, sharing, and trust within an atmosphere of informality. Even in the small groups of our larger, secular society, Wuthnow says, formality must come first: "The paradox . . . is genuine: the informality of small groups depends on having formal structure, and the formal structure is tolerated only because of the informality it encourages." Formal structures in small groups, Wuthnow goes on to say, "create a space for people to get to know each other. Trust can develop more easily because people do not have to worry much about group goals."

Small Group Ministry has an inherent goal: satisfying the human need for ultimacy and intimacy. For us, the paradox Wuthnow identifies is that a structure and a format are required if we are to create the informal communities most of us want to make available to more than just an inner circle of "family" members.

How many people come to our churches in the hope of learning what our formal educations have taught us? Few or perhaps none. How many people will respond with joy and gratitude to the chance to be heard respectfully in small groups of intelligent, caring, religiously liberal people? Far more—perhaps more than we've ever before dreamed of serving. Giving people a chance, then, to speak of their life journeys in circumstances that build mutual trust is our goal, and the best ways of reaching that goal involve study, careful planning, and the full implementation of the structures of Small Group Ministries.

Choosing, Appointing and Training Facilitators

The work of covenant group facilitators can be simple and easy, but at times it becomes complex and difficult. Wuthnow, in his study of small groups of all varieties, calls attention to both the simplicity and the centrality of facilitation. "It does not take a great deal of special knowledge or skill to make a small group function well," he says. But then he adds, "Groups can be badly misled. They can certainly fall apart from mismanagement." Therefore, we expect more from covenant group facilitators than we normally expect of volunteers, and we offer them more as well.

The usual practice in Unitarian Universalist congregations, Roger Comstock wrote in a newsletter column while he was serving as interim district minister in the Northeast District, is to "beat the bushes" of the congregation to find someone willing to assume leadership of a committee, thank them profusely for agreeing to take on the responsibility, announce their agreement to serve, and then forget about them until it is time for a committee report to the annual meeting of the church. The results, in many of our societies, are ineffectiveness, committees of one, and a lot of frustration. Still, it is something else again, he continued, for us to be using a covenant group system that carefully selects someone; trains that person; provides that person with definite guidelines, including a recommendation for frequency of meetings and a meeting format to follow; and requires that person to meet regularly with the minister and others doing similar work in the church.

Will Unitarian Universalists accept enough rules to make small group organization work? Covenants, frequent meetings that start and end on time and use a prescribed format, and appointed facilitators may seem like a lot to ask. The fact that so many of us have so readily adopted these constraints, however, is due to the fact that once the basic structure is accepted, the group has freedom constrained only by the boundaries of the congregation's culture and purpose. Freedom within small groups, Wuthnow says, "must be supported zealously."

The rapid spread of these methods may also indicate how far we've come from the radical individualism that has sometimes characterized Unitarian Universalism. "Small groups need to be encouraged to behave as groups rather than as aggregates of individuals," Wuthnow observes. In *The Devotional Heart,* John Morgan urges us to see ourselves as "a community, a people, and not simply as individuals who gather on Sunday." The presence of covenant group facilitators in our congregations, a new designation for a differently empowered leader, may both indicate how our congregations have changed in recent years and, at the same time, provide a leadership model for our future.

The title *facilitator* reflects the fact that the individual must be capable of making covenant group membership easier by attending to the procedural and relational aspects of the group. One experienced Small Group Ministry advocate, Diana Dorroh of Baton Rouge, Louisiana, cautions, correctly, that sometimes the facilitator has to lead. As an example, she cites a situation in which a facilitator allowed a group to abandon key elements of covenant group procedure. What he facilitated was his group's ceasing to be, in fact, a covenant group. Within the normal boundaries of covenant group functioning, though, there is more need for flexibility and ease than for rigid control. Good facilitators lead lightly. Dame has said, "The facilitator guides with a gentle hand, and often does not even lead every meeting."

Dr. Mellen Kennedy's 1995 doctoral dissertation focused on mutual help groups. As a part of the Center for Community Values (CCV), Kennedy took part in a "Practitioners' Summit" in March, 2001, at Countryside Church in Palatine, Illinois. At this CCV-sponsored gathering of Small Group Ministry leaders, she stressed the sharing of leadership that facilitators need to encourage:

> Shared ministry operates through shared leadership. . . . Participants need to feel, "This is our group," not the facilitator's group. The clearer you have the ground rules, the clearer the covenant, the clearer the format that is used, then the more anybody and everybody will feel that they can help facilitate. People develop more of a sense of democracy and a sense of ownership. We

should be aiming to encourage facilitators to work for shared leadership, shared facilitation, so they don't always have to be in control.

Wuthnow agrees. The "secret of the small-group movement's success," he says, is in the emphasis on smallness, informality, and personal interaction, which has allowed members to feel important. "They can take pride in their groups, experience a sense of ownership, and gain satisfaction when the group functions well."

Finding and Selecting Facilitators

Where can a minister or a lay leader of a congregation find enough people willing to meet once or twice a month to facilitate an experience for others and, in addition, meet regularly, perhaps once a month, with the minister or the covenant group spokesperson? Three meetings a month, perhaps? Nine or more hours out of every month for church work? And think how many of these folks you are going to need!

Turner says that many of our churches live in "institutional survival mode" because their leaders believe the following "persistent myths": there are too few people for too many tasks in our churches, and busy, modern-day people have no time for church work. In *Transforming Our Churches with Small Group Ministry*, Turner says that acting as if these myths are true saps the energies of leaders and accounts for much of the unrewarding nature of most church efforts. Our traditional methods of managing our churches have left too many of us poorly served. Turner writes, "When we're not getting what we came for (spiritual inspiration, community, religious growth), then what we do in the service of the church is tiring. Being fed spiritually and communally is energizing. When things are going well, people have time to participate without complaint."

Much of our Small Group Ministry experience thus far supports this view. "Finally, we're getting something back," deeply involved leaders of Cleveland's West Shore congregation told McGee at the end of the pilot covenant group he led for them. A renewal of spirit, energy, and willingness to serve results from covenant group involvement.

After clarifying goals and purposes and after understanding thoroughly what Small Group Ministry is, identifying people most likely to facilitate well is probably the most important prelaunch task. Once the program is under way, leaders need to constantly be scanning the available pool of potential facilitators because a successful program will produce the need for more groups and, therefore, more facilitators.

Facilitator selection is not a popularity contest and should not be done by majority vote of the board or congregation. When the church has a minister or ministers, the selection of facilitators should be their responsibility. Small Group Ministry asks the called, professional minister to share his or her ministry, so that minister must feel comfortable with each and every facilitator. The minister must be able to work well, sometimes in situations requiring the keeping of confidence, with all facilitators. Lacking the wisdom and stature of Solomon (not to mention the protection afforded by being, like Solomon, long-since dead), ministers may be wise to have an advisory committee of lay leaders with whom to consult.

When there is no minister, a board-appointed committee of three lay folks may be best. The fellowship's board should make it clear that these three (or two or one) individuals are authorized to make decisions and that they have the full backing of the board. It will usually be best, though, for just one person—called the *Small Group Ministry czar,* for want of a better term—to speak for the decision-making group. The czar and her or his committee should be empowered to make all the selections, including the difficult ones, that would belong to the minister, if a minister were in place. By making these decisions carefully, the small decision-making group will be helping the fellowship fulfill its ministry to its members, including those already on the rolls and those yet to be welcomed.

Persuading people to be facilitators or facilitators-in-training can be problematic, too. Sometimes people fear they are not qualified. Brent Smith said in a conference call workshop sponsored by *Covenant Group News,* with tongue partly in cheek, "Never ask a professor or teacher to be a facilitator. They'll treat the group like a class." He exaggerates to make the point that the facilitator does not have to be an expert or a content provider. Dame says something similar in his *Resource Book*: "Small Group Ministry is neither therapy nor a course in religion. . . . Good commonsense, which is actually pretty common in our congregations, is the strongest qualification."

Apprentices and Cofacilitators

The model of Small Group Ministry applied in Augusta, Maine, involves having both a facilitator and a facilitator-in-training, or apprentice, in each group. This model was not always in place when the program was just getting started. In the early days, a facilitator resigned from a group that had no apprentice. The transition was difficult. Dame and his lay leaders decided that in the future, they would have apprentices ready to step in when facilitators left their positions. And Dame sees a second reason for having apprentices. In his *Resource Book* he writes,

> They are the key to the expansion of a small group program. New groups require leadership, and the people who understand the promise and the process of Small Group Ministry are the people in the groups. As new people become intrigued and ready to join a group, an apprentice graduates to be the facilitator for a new group, or stays with the existing group while the facilitator pulls a new group together. And it might be that one or two of the existing group goes along with the facilitator or apprentice to the new group just to help form a core of ministry.

Some congregations are experimenting with cofacilitators. The Unitarian Church of Baton Rouge has used cofacilitators, including at least one married couple. Vaeni, of the Olympia, Washington, Unitarian Universalist congregation, says his church chose cofacilitators over the facilitator-and-apprentice model in order to "swap responsibility from one meeting to the next or share parts of meetings or share the whole meeting." Only one facilitator from each group is expected to attend the monthly facilitators' meeting, but, Vaeni says, "Most of them appreciate both the camaraderie and the sharing they experience at the [Facilitators' Group] meetings, so most of them try to attend each meeting."

Training Facilitators

Can facilitators be trained in a single session? The first six covenant group facilitators in Dame's church had all taken part in planning their program as members of the Small Group Ad Hoc Planning Committee, so Dame's initial training for them was carried out in a single evening. In his *Resource Book,* Dame explains, "I put up newsprint and asked them what their fears were. We put those on the newsprint, and by the time we finished talking about them, none of them seemed overwhelming. We then discussed a covenant of mutual support and support for the vision of the Small Group Ministry Program."

The amount of training needed depends, of course, on the people selected to be facilitators. "If somebody's not very good at this, you can't train them in a weekend," Robinson said at the CCV Practitioners' Summit, adding that he tries to find facilitators who are natural leaders and "only need orientation," not training.

Whether through orientation or training, McGee's way of preparing facilitators to begin working with covenant groups takes place between the hours of 9:00 A.M. and 12 noon on Saturdays at the Unitarian Universalist Church of Arlington, Virginia. McGee found the demand for covenant groups there so great that he and his cominister, Gelbine, decided to begin facilitator training within six months of McGee's arrival in 1999—much sooner than he had planned. McGee said at the practitioners summit, "We decided to go into fast mode. We selected folks who were very excited about being asked to be facilitators. We had one training session. We started with six groups right off the bat."

Behind the belief that brief training can be adequate for covenant group facilitators lies this fundamental assumption: Most training of facilitators will be ongoing, taking place in facilitators' covenant groups. Meeting with other facilitators and the minister or appointed Small Group Ministry czar once a month, facilitators will be able to experience being in (as opposed to being responsible for) a covenant group while having a chance to raise questions and address concerns growing out of their experiences as facilitators. In a message he sends to facilitators prior to their training sessions, McGee says,

> An important part of the ongoing training [will be] taking part in a facilitators' covenant group led by the ministers. The purpose of such a group is (1) to allow leaders to have the opportunity to experience the support and challenge of groups as a participant, (2) to develop leadership skills, and (3) to use other leaders and the ministers to help resolve problems.

Asked about his monthly meetings with facilitators, Dame responded,

> We consult on questions which arise from time to time. The facilitators' meeting with me encourages a sense of ministry within their group, keeping people informed of events or concerns, and encouraging expressions of caring. And, with appropriate permission, they alert me to situations where my presence or attention as minister might be needed.

These regular meetings of facilitators with the minister (or in fellowships, with the Small Group Ministry czar) are also one of our ways of protecting against error or incompetence. Because we are putting in place shared ministries, we need to ask our facilitators to agree to uphold the same sort of basic, ethical guidelines that ministers agree to uphold. At a minimum, facilitators should be asked to affirm the following commitment adapted from the Code of Professional Practices of the Unitarian Universalist Ministers' Association (changes are shown in brackets): "I will remember that a congregation places special trust in its [shared ministry] leadership and that the members of [covenant groups may] allow a [facilitator] to become a part of their lives on the basis of that trust. I will not abuse or exploit that trust for my own gratification."

Training facilitators, though, soon may not be enough. McGee is looking ahead to training trainers of facilitators. After a little more than a year, the Arlington Church covenant group program had grown to 18 groups with 150 participants, and new groups were being added at the rate of about one per month. Finding and training new facilitators to keep pace with the growth of groups, McGee says, continues to take significant time and effort. Soon additional helpers may be required. McGee is looking ahead to the time when his job will be training those who will train facilitators. While he and several other Unitarian Universalist ministers were listening to Dale Galloway, author and president of a seminary in Kentucky, speak about his use of the Willow Creek or meta-church model of small group organization in building a church in Oregon, McGee felt that he was getting an insight into some changes ahead:

> He built up that church, a Christian church, from nothing to 6,500. As he was speaking to this group of Unitarian Universalist ministers, it just dawned on me that we were like a kindergarten class with this professor speaking to us. He does not have a Unitarian Universalist bone in his body, but this guy and his colleagues know how to build churches. And they do it with small groups. The only way to do it is to train leaders to train leaders. This is our future.

Some Messages for Facilitators

The Arlington church plan, simple though it may seem to people accustomed to the training of leaders for therapy groups, is compatible with the elements deemed most important by Thom Corrigan and Richard Pearce, authors of *Learning to Care: Developing Community in Small Groups.* Corrigan and Pearce say that if the facilitators are well-respected members with good relational skills, they need only be people who are

- willing to meet once a month or more with their groups;
- willing to implement the small group approach and rituals; and
- aware of the difference between leading a meeting and facilitating a meeting.

A few items might be added to the core understandings required of covenant group facilitators. Facilitators should know the following in beginning their work, or be taught these things before they start facilitating a group:

- The recommended format, beginning with a reading and a check-in and ending with a reading and a check-out, is central to every covenant group's success.
- Covenant groups are different from other small groups.
- Covenant group facilitation is not the same as the leadership of committees, the teaching of classes, or other roles they may be accustomed to filling.
- Covenant groups are shared ministry.
- Three kinds of covenants will contribute to the covenant group's health: the group's agreement on how members will interact with one another, the commitment to serve the congregation as a group at least once each year, and the covenant to find and participate together in at least two community-improvement projects.

Practical Matters

One should not assume that facilitators in training have thought through the practical details of covenant group facilitation. Some recommendations and the reasoning behind them follow:

Start and stop the meetings on time. If you do, people will become more prompt, and they'll take comfort in knowing the meeting will end when it is supposed to end. Prompt meeting endings can be especially important for evening meetings, when people may need to return to their own homes by a fixed time.

Do not promise confidentiality. Suggest, instead, that the group's covenant of interactions include something like "In what we say both inside and outside this group, we will seek to avoid gossip or speaking disrespectfully to or about each other." Promises of strict confidentiality are not likely to be kept in a group that will be welcoming new members and seeing others move on; in addition, confidentiality is associated with support groups and therapy groups, which are different in both leadership and structure from covenant groups. Also, because this is shared ministry, situations may arise in which the facilitator needs the freedom to communicate to others, in a responsible, ministerial manner, information from covenant group sessions.

Discourage food or beverages. With the exception, of course, of affinity groups involving food (the Cooking with Turnips Covenant Group, perhaps), Small Group Ministries should be free of the distractions that frequently accompany snacks or beverages. A major appeal of covenant groups is that they require almost no preparation, from session to session, on anyone's part. That positive characteristic is lost if someone has to be responsible for buying or preparing snacks. Covenant groups don't need the social lubrication of food or drinks.

Don't allow cross-talk. Establish the expectation of withholding all but the briefest of responses during check-in until everyone has had the chance to speak.

Urge people to be slow about giving advice. Listening and understanding what participants say is a gift. Ready advice is not usually perceived to be a gift. Covenant groups are more about acceptance and understanding than about problem solving.

Encourage participants not to expect resolution. The time allotted will rarely be enough for the group to reach consensus, finish a task, or resolve an issue. The richer a topic turns out to be for a particular group, the more likely it will be that a facilitator will have to interrupt to do the always-needed closing check-out and reading. This should not be viewed as a problem.

Remember that the point is learning, not teaching. In covenant groups, learning about one another is usually more important than conveying information about the topic of the meeting. Even if the focus is on existentialism, for example, an explication of Sartre's impact on modern philosophy, however astute, will be out of place. More to the point may be a story about how reading Sartre influenced one's life.

Recognize that facilitating good process matters more than providing content. The facilitator's responsibility for providing covenant group meeting content is minimal. Through session plans or sermons, ministers may provide discussion-starter material. Sometimes, the content is inherent in the covenant group's focus and reason for coming together. A covenant group for quilters, for example, will need opening and closing readings, but their main focus will be on quilting (and as fingers sew, conversation will flow). When a facilitator does feel the need to provide some discussion-opening material, it is often enough to ask group members to reflect on the meaning, for them, of a single word (*trust, courage,* or *hope,* for example). Generally, members generate their own content, even when something more formal is provided. One covenant group facilitator told me, "It doesn't matter much what our topic is. We read a sentence or two from something, the discussion takes off, and we never get back to what we started with."

Expect to ask a lot of questions. Questions are a primary tool for encouraging others to participate. If individuals are not participating in the discussion, ask (nonpushy) follow-up questions to draw them in—for example, "John, how would you respond to that?" or "Does anybody who hasn't spoken yet have a reflection on what has just been said?" Questions may be useful even when someone has gone off on a tangent that others appear uninterested in following. One might ask, for example, "And how is this relevant to our topic tonight?"

Model answers, sometimes. Providing answers is not normally the facilitator's role, but it may occasionally be useful for a facilitator to model the sort of response being sought. If you've suggested starting with each person giving a two-minute answer to the question "How has tonight's topic been important in my life?" you might demonstrate good practice by going first, being careful to speak from your own experience rather than reporting on your reading about the topic or what you've heard from others. In addition, be sure to speak for only two minutes or less.

If a member is missing, find out why. If a member has not let someone know the reason for an absence, that member should get a call from the facilitator, the apprentice, or someone acting in their behalf no later than the next day. A common complaint in our congregations is, "I was not there, and nobody cared." Small Group Ministries should never provide grounds for that complaint.

Be the keeper of the covenant. Welcome help with the task of constantly recalling the group's behavioral covenant, but remember that it is your responsibility, if no one else takes it, to call attention gently (and finally, if necessary, firmly) to the agreed-upon ways of relating in the group. When a new person joins the group, introducing that person to the group's covenant at the beginning of the meeting should be the facilitator's job if he or she has not delegated it to another member of the group. (At the start of the new person's second meeting, he or she should be asked to either affirm the covenant or suggest the consideration of changes to it.)

Difficult Members

A question raised so often that it deserves its own heading is, How do we deal with difficult members? That's a scary question for us and, judging by the literature on small group organization, for others as well. Many writers speak of problematic covenant group members as *extra-grace-required people*. George uses the term *extra-care-needed members*. Some folks can give even professionally led therapy groups fits. Small Group Ministry, though, gives us some tools for responding. One *CGNews* reader wrote, "If your experience is like mine, you know that one deeply needy person can kill a whole group. We have a couple in our small groups, but this covenant group process, as simple as it seems, has turned out to be wonderfully strong. There has been some turbulence, but so far no damage."

Each group's covenant, created and owned by the members, is an important tool available to the facilitator as a source of authority whenever someone in the group begins behaving in a way that is contrary to the group's well-considered agreements. Kennedy's doctoral dissertation work put her in touch with small groups serving a population of more than a hundred people, all suffering from mental illness. "These groups were wonderful and people's lives were transformed in them," Kennedy says, and she attributes their success to two factors: strong facilitation and clear, explicit ground rules. "You need really clear ground rules and strong, shared facilitation to keep extra-grace people on track behaviorally," she believes, so that either the facilitator or a group member is free to say things like "Sally, our ground rule is that we don't attack people."

Should a member ever be asked to leave? Possibly, yes. If a member is unable or unwilling to abide by the covenant, then the facilitator needs to protect the group from debilitating disruption. At such a point, the minister, caring committee of the church, or both should be informed and might need to become involved. At the same time, we should also be clear that we are engaged in shared ministry. Dame reminds people of that reality, sometimes, when he hears complaints about difficult people in his church's Small Group Ministries. At the CCV Practitioners' Summit, Dame reported that he has told people the following: "Well, you know, ministry's not always easy. Ministry is more about what we have to give than about what we get back. We have to be patient. I don't always get to minister just to the people I like. My job is to minister to anybody who walks in the front door." Usually, he says, group members respond by settling back and going to work, doing ministry.

The Rewards of Facilitating

We should not overemphasize the possibility of problems with difficult folk. Far more common than tales of distress seem to be stories like the one Dame told during the CCV Practitioners' Summit. A longtime member of his Augusta congregation, Bill Galbraith, had held many positions in the church, including being finance chair and serving on the buildings and grounds committee, when he let Dame know that he wanted to move away from that sort of work and become, instead, a covenant group facilitator. Dame appointed him, and after Galbraith had been facilitating a successful Small Group Ministry for a while, he asked Galbraith to accompany him and some other lay folk to a meeting to introduce leaders of other churches to covenant groups. When it was his time to speak at that meeting, Galbraith's words moved his minister. Galbraith said,

> After years of doing all those different jobs in the church, I really wanted to work on something more spiritual, more connected. Now, within my church, I have my own little neighborhood to take care of. I have my small garden to tend, my neighborhood to care for and nurture. We have our ups and downs and ups again, and it is just wonderful.

Dame cited this story as an illustration of what can happen when there is genuinely shared ministry in a church. People who are perceived, like Galbraith, to be practical, nuts-and-bolts, buildings-and-grounds, finance-chair sorts of people can turn out to be nurturers, effective and caring gardeners of others, when we, as Dame said, "invite them to do something that is 'church,' something that is spiritual, when we empower them to minister in the context of lay ministry in the life of the church." When, in other words, we invite someone to be a covenant group facilitator.

Three Kinds of Covenants

Save the world or savor it? Some say that question is a daily dilemma of living a responsible life. Sometimes, though, our choices are necessarily more self-focused. Just getting through the day often seems to be as much as we can manage. Our appreciation of the world doesn't rise to the level of savoring the sound of falling rain, the presence of friends and family, or the gift of being able to lift a hand to wave hello or goodbye. Saving the world is not on our day's "to-do" list.

"Saving the world" is a grandiose phrase. It points to the far end of a continuum of impulses that move from pure self-interest outward. Attending to those people emotionally closest to us is one step along that continuum. Caring about our neighbor is another, and fulfilling the responsibilities of citizenship is one more.

What will be the effects of our years spent breathing, making choices, being human on this small planet we've now become able to see from space? As noted earlier, Unitarian Universalists on their deathbeds have deplored the failure of their churches to help them share with others the stories of life journeys or to provide opportunities to talk with others about what is of greatest value. What regrets might we have when we look back on the roles we played in our churches and the roles our churches played in the world?

Small Group Ministry asks us not only to attend to the stresses of getting through the day but also to covenant together to do what we can to make a positive difference. A faith statement is implied in those two purposes. We covenant to be generous with each other and to work for positive change because we have faith that some finite number of people, consciously working to make a difference, can literally save the world from the hoard of well-envisioned devastations that may be lying in wait for us all and for our earth. Through three types of promises made in community—a behavioral covenant, a covenant with the congregation, and a covenant to serve the larger community—Small Group Ministry asks us to affirm meaning and purpose.

A Behavioral Covenant

We use the word *covenant* to mean "a binding agreement made by two or more parties." That is the first definition in *Webster's New College Dictionary.* For us the term *binding* means "binding until the group decides to amend this covenant," and it has no legalistic intent. Similarly, we use *covenant* without reference to Judeo-Christian debates about covenants between Yahweh and Israel in Old Testament lore or Christian claims of a new covenant through Jesus Christ. Some Unitarian Universalists dislike the term *covenant,* but we've found no term that is objection-free and *covenant* carries the useful connotation of being a bit more considered, more deliberate, than *promise,* the closest synonym for what we mean to say.

The first covenant of Small Group Ministry is one the group members make to one another. We begin with a behavioral covenant, an agreement about how the group's members wish to be together. While arriving at this agreement could be the first task of the first meeting after the opening and the check-in, our experience indicates that it is better for the group to have one or two meetings together before attempting to agree on a covenant.

A facilitator, in telling the group that the "business" of the second or third meeting will be the creation of a behavioral covenant, gives members time to consider what they think should be included. Sometimes a meeting or two without a covenant offers object lessons in why the covenant is important. One facilitator said, "After our first meeting was dominated by a talker, I knew the group was going to insist on agreements about sharing time equally when we got to the discussion of our covenant."

Facilitators sometimes offer sample covenants borrowed from other groups as guidelines for their own group's considerations. Worries that Unitarian Universalists will have difficulty agreeing on how they want to be together, however, seem to be largely misplaced. Despite our sometimes undisciplined behavior in large gatherings, when we gather in someone's living room in a covenant group, we seem to have a clear and largely shared understanding of behaviors that are fair and generous.

It may be best for a facilitator to offer a series of questions that suggest the issues normally addressed in small group covenants, leaving the response to those questions to the group's own creativity. The questions most often dealt with in covenant formation include the following:

Arrangements
- Where shall we meet? (In some instances, the meeting place may have been determined already. The facilitator may have chosen to use her or his home, for example.)
- When shall we meet, and for how long? (This too may have been predetermined and made a part of the announcement and sign-up sheet.)
- Shall we sit, as nearly as possible, in a circle with all, including any latecomers, included?

Respect for one another's time
- Do we agree to arrive by a stated time? How many minutes early is it okay for us to arrive?
- Do we agree to start the meeting at the announced starting time, or is it our plan to start later than we say we're going to?
- Do we agree to stop each meeting by the announced ending time? Under what circumstances would we make exceptions to that? Are we free to hang around for unstructured visiting after the meeting? If so, for how many minutes? (Sensitivity to the needs of the host or hostess would be important here.)

Commitment to attend
- Do we agree to make every attempt to attend each meeting?
- Do we agree to let someone know in advance if we are going to have to be absent?

Sharing "airtime"
- How much time do we want to allot to each person for check-in? How much time for check-out?
- If someone has a need for a longer time to check in, how do we decide to allow more time?
- Do we agree to refrain from commenting on what people say during check-in until all of us have had the chance to check in?

- Do we agree to monitor our own vocalizations to be sure that time is shared equitably?
- Shall we use a "talking stick" or other symbol to remind ourselves of who has the floor at any given moment?
- Shall we agree not to interrupt the person holding the talking stick?

General respect
- Shall we encourage people to speak from their own experiences rather than from what they've read or what they theorize?
- Shall we focus our remarks, as much as possible, on the here and now rather than dwelling on past concerns or future speculations?
- Shall we discourage advice giving?
- Shall we avoid criticizing others while allowing for the critical consideration of ideas and beliefs?
- Shall we be guided, in our decision making, by the purposes of our church and the Unitarian Universalist Association?
- Do we agree to reconsider this covenant whenever one of us or a new member asks for a reconsideration of any of these provisions?

Service to others
- Shall we always have one empty chair in our circle to remind ourselves that there are others who need what we have found here?
- Shall we agree to spawn another group whenever our membership reaches eight or ten?
- Shall we agree to find at least one way each year, as a group, to serve our church?
- Shall we agree to find at least two ways each year, as a group, to serve our larger community?

The facilitator
- Shall we authorize our facilitator (and cofacilitator or apprentice) to call us back to this covenant of mutual respect and considerate behavior whenever he or she believes we have strayed from it?

Once the basic structure and concept of Small Group Ministry is accepted, of course, the group has total freedom, within the normal confines of Unitarian Universalist church life, to make any decisions it wishes. A covenant group's members may decide not to start on time, not to end at a preannounced time, and not to bother attending unless they feel like it. They'll probably call their covenant group something like the "Non-compulsives" and feel proud of their counter-cultural spirit. They will have the right to do that, and their group's life span will probably be short.

A Covenant with the Congregation

In one church, an all-female group that had grown out of a religious education program focused on women's issues voted to close its meetings and announced that decision in the church's newsletter. Other women in the congregation protested. They spoke in various words a single message: "No women's group holding meetings in my church should be closed to me." Rather than reverse their decision, the "Cakes for the Queen of Heaven" group moved its meetings to the homes of members. Few members of the group attended church services after that, and within a few months they all had disappeared from church activities.

As useful as "Cakes" groups were for many when they flourished in some of our congregations, they lacked sufficient connection to the churches that sponsored them. More than one floated away, taking valued church members with them. Memories of such loses have caused some of us to be cautious, on first exposure, about covenant groups. People fear cliques, and rightly so (except, of course, the people comfortably near the center of them). Several elements work against cliquishness in Small Group Ministry.

One protection is that all the rules, rituals, and procedures of Small Group Ministry are made explicit. They are publicly stated and written down. They are equally available to everyone, newcomer and old-timer alike. Cliques, by contrast, have implicit rules—requirements for admission that are not publicly stated. For the most part, one has to be invited into a clique. All that is required of anyone wanting to take part in Small Group Ministry is that he or she say so to the appropriate (and publicly identified) person.

Another protection against cliquishness and divisiveness is the facilitator, a carefully chosen person who meets regularly with other facilitators and the minister or Small Group Ministry czar. Any tendency toward separatism that might develop in a covenant group would surface in the facilitators' covenant group discussions, and a means could be found to remind the group of their purpose and function as a part of the church.

The third protection is the expectation that each covenant group will, as a group, perform at least one service for the congregation each year. This service to the church will serve as a reminder of the group's relationship with the rest of the congregation. A surprise benefit of serving the church as a group is that folks tend to enjoy the experience. One covenant group in a nonministered fellowship agreed to present a Sunday service. The creation and presentation of this worship service met their annual obligation, but working together in that way gave them so much pleasure that they also volunteered to clean up after coffee hour every Sunday for a month.

Having the group covenant to do something at least once a year for the congregation as a whole can be an effective way of introducing nonmembers to our churches. Our covenant groups need to be back-door entries into the church community for potential members. Sometimes people ask if it is okay to invite people who are not members of the church to join a covenant group. The answer is, Yes, of course! It is our hope that Unitarian Universalists will find it easier to invite people to a meeting about a topic or activity of mutual interest than to invite them to a Sunday service, and that those invited will be able to get the best possible introduction to our faith in two steps:

- First, they will come to know and become friends with some Unitarian Universalists. Churches of all denominations find that personal acquaintance with someone already a member greatly increases the likelihood that a visitor will stay and join.
- Second, they will participate in planning to do something each year for the church and then participate in that activity. If nothing else has, this will get them through the sometimes-intimidating front door.

In addition, they will have heard at least two readings, each meeting, from Unitarian Universalist sources or sources at least compatible with the goals and purposes of the sponsoring church and Unitarian Universalism.

Of course, no covenant group member should be pressured to become a member of the church. The invitation to join should be extended, but a person not likely ever to become Unitarian Universalist may well be a valued part of a covenant group indefinitely. As a part of the covenant group, the person will be asked to serve the church in some way at least once a year, and the invitation to membership can remain unobtrusively open.

Covenant to Serve the Larger Community

In our culture today, Wuthnow has found, the ability of small groups to cultivate community often comes not only from encouraging folks to share their thoughts and interests within their groups but also from prompting people "to become more active in their communities, to help others who may be in need, and to think more deeply about pressing social and political issues." Service, both to the sponsoring congregation and to the larger community, is a vital and often infectiously enlivening aspect of many Unitarian Universalist Small Group Ministries.

Jim Robinson, the minister of the First Parish in Brewster, Massachusetts, who has been using Small Group Ministry techniques since 1982, finds that covenant groups and/or affinity groups account for most of the social justice work of his church. Small Group Ministry can provide effort-sustaining support to individuals doing social justice work. At the CCV Practitioners Summit, Robinson said,

> If you're working on a project that can be accomplished in four or five months, maybe you can do it on your own. But if the change you want to bring about is going to take longer than that, you need a covenant group. You need a small group to come back to, a place to tell stories, discuss strategy, get your wounds tended, and get your batteries re-charged so you can go out again.

These Small Group Ministry benefits are similar to the benefits Wuthnow finds in small groups everywhere that encourage private beliefs to find expression in public acts: "holding each other accountable, stepping in when personal discipline weakens, providing mentoring, and nurturing each other toward greater insight and mutual responsibility."

Perhaps Small Group Ministry can provide religious liberals an antidote to a disturbing tendency in local and regional social issue debates: Individuals who take positions generally opposite to ours tend to be more persistent. Sustained by firmly held, dogmatic beliefs, they tend to be around even after those on our side of the debates have moved on to something else. The success of the Brewster church's covenant group approach offers hope that Small Group Ministry might help us change that politically costly dynamic. In addition to being a primary outreach success in our Association, Robinson's church has helped bring significant social changes to the area. Several of the church's covenant groups, for example, have focused on the concerns of mothers on welfare, and others have worked for fair employment benefits for homosexual couples. The result? Our Brewster church is known to others in the region as "the conscience of Cape Cod."

The Literacy Covenant Group at the Bay Area Community Church in Houston is focused on providing friendship, information, and support to tutors of children and adults in that community who speak English poorly or not at all. Making church members aware of community programs needing their help is one function of this covenant group, according to Paula Criswell, facilitator. Another function is encouraging church members to act on that awareness. In a newsletter article seeking tutors of English as a second language for adults, Criswell writes,

> Do you have an hour or two a week to give to someone who needs your help? Many of our neighbors struggle every day to get by in a world we take for granted. They miss out on better jobs, important information, potential friends, and many other things because they can't speak English. You may be saying, "I'd like to help, but I'm not qualified." Can you speak English? Do you have a couple of hours a week to spare? Do you have a willing heart to help make life better for someone eager to learn? If so, with minimal training, you're qualified!

Criswell says her covenant group is "a wonderful medium for building friendships among like-minded people" and that it has another reason for being: to help church members fulfill the congregation's purpose. "Every Sunday," she notes, "we recite our Unison Affirmation. In one line we covenant with one another 'To serve humanity in fellowship.'"

Although there are glorious exceptions, probably only a few of our Small Group Ministries have fulfilled their commitments to work as groups in their larger communities. Bruce R. Russell-Jayne, who has been a covenant group facilitator at the Unitarian Universalist Church of Chattanooga, Tennessee, recently e-mailed a question to *Covenant Group News*: "How do you get covenant groups into social justice work? Our groups love to talk, but none of them have been motivated to work." Perhaps Small Group Ministry, which is, after all, still new to us, will mature into stronger outward commitments as time goes on. It may be that our covenant groups go though adolescent-like phases of self-focus and that time is required for the maturity of other-focus to grow stronger. That would explain the reluctance of some groups to change by adding new members or to reconfigure in order to birth new groups, as well as our slowness to engage larger-community activities.

We are not the only religious group struggling with these issues, of course. Michael C. Mack, small groups minister at the Foothills Christian Church in Boise, Idaho, asked in an on-line newsletter recently whether the many thousands of small groups in Christian churches are making any difference:

> Are all these groups . . . really changing the cultural landscape of our country? Shouldn't they? . . . Caring for one another, encouraging one another, serving one another is a good thing. But when it remains inward-focused, it is not really a Christian thing. . . . When small groups begin to touch and redeem the neighborhoods around them, then replicating that and multiplying it over and over again, we really will begin to transform our country—and our world—for Christ!

Time may bring maturity to our Small Group Ministries, and this maturity may be expressed through participation in twice-a-year community-betterment projects. Until active altruism kicks in, though, groups might find self-interest motivation in the experience of covenant groups in Arlington, Virginia. At the CCV Practitioners Summit, McGee said that when a facilitator complains to him that a covenant group is getting stale or losing energy, he has ready advice: "Get your group involved in a service project." So far, that advice has produced the desired results. "It's amazing," he says, "the leaders always come back saying, 'Wow, we're all charged up again.'"

Right Relationship

Our covenants to each other, to our churches, and to our larger communities promote the two main goals of Small Group Ministry: saving the world and getting through our days. The two goals are deeply intertwined, of course. Our feelings about our lives on the mundane, day-to-day level are deeply influenced by our sense of ourselves as being in community and contributing to the welfare of others, including future generations of human beings. Further, concern for humans necessarily implies concern for the other living entities that form, as our Purposes and Principles say, the web of all existence of which we are a part. We want our lives and our religion to count for something on the scales of justice and on behalf of ecological sustainability.

Our covenants remind us of the importance of working together and being in community. With some reason, we Unitarian Universalists have worried that our critics are right to see us as too inward focused. By emphasizing all three types of covenants inherent in Small Group Ministry, we free ourselves from that charge. Wuthnow says:

> Faced by the prospect of piety turning increasingly inward, religious leaders can take comfort in the fact that small groups—perhaps more than anything else—encourage private beliefs to be shared publicly and to be acted on in ways that others can see. Giving voice to one's religious views in a small group is certainly a more open, dynamic process than listening to sermon on Sunday morning. . . . And working within a small group to feed the hungry and clothe the naked is certainly a "corporate" expression of faith to a greater extent than offering a silent prayer for the needy or dropping a check in the mail.

Covenant groups do not provide us with a particular political agenda, liberal or conservative. They are content neutral in format. As Wuthnow says, "Small groups make a difference primarily by supporting individuals, by helping them lead their lives more effectively, and by nurturing individual-level contacts that may lead to action of some kind on a larger scale." The services we perform as covenant groups of Unitarian Universalist congregations, however, do take place within the context of liberal religious beliefs, including the inherent worth and dignity of all. In the bloodstream of our faith is the optimistic Universalist belief in the eventual salvation of all souls. Many of us have experienced the wisdom that can come, in the safety of small groups, from the sharing of differing viewpoints based on varied experiences. And sometimes that wisdom moves us to act, in consort with others. "Spirituality in small groups," Wuthnow finds, "for all its diversity, is very much a collective enterprise."

"Covenant group work is a this-world ministry that heals," says Thandeka, associate professor of theology and culture at Meadville/Lombard Theological School, Chicago. By encouraging right relationships within our groups and within our larger communities, she told workshop participants at a recent General Assembly, covenant group work focuses on the healing of both individuals and their communities: "This is spiritual work: the experience of being healed, of being loved and, thus, of finding a life of meaningful, open-hearted relationships that both honor and respect one's self, others, and the world."

Expanding Circles and Welcoming New Friends

Consider these facts: People bond quickly and with surprising ease in covenant groups; once a successful Small Group Ministry is established, more and more people decide they want to be part of a covenant group; and virtually everyone agrees that covenant group bonding happens best in, and perhaps only in, groups of no more than eight, ten, or (at the absolute maximum) twelve. This combination of covenant group characteristics leads to amoeba-like growth.

Because people bond quickly in covenant groups and the joys of being in a covenant group begin to drop away when membership approaches ten or so, the members of any covenant group nearing the maximum size for effectiveness will be glad to send the group's apprentice or cofacilitator and two or three of its newest members off to form a new group. That will open space for additional members, and the newcomers will be seamlessly assimilated into their new covenant group community. Furthermore, the original group will follow with parentlike pride the progress of the group they've spun off. Thus, covenant groups will grow, divide, and begin again, generation after generation, with relative ease, and all will be well, right?

Wrong. Our experience so far is that covenant groups form, grow, and resist the amoeba step. "Once people have found what they have a burning desire for, they don't want to let it go," Cheryl Ring, a lay member of our Augusta, Maine, congregation said at the CCV Practitioners Summit. She then identified the catch-22 of covenant group success: "We found that what small-group ministry offers is what people want. So we're successful. Because our groups are so successful, we can't split them." Her minister, Calvin Dame, agreed. So did Robinson, dean of the gathering, whose experience stretches back to 1982. McGee says he ran into "a massive rebellion" in his Virginia congregation when he urged groups to solve their size problems by dividing off new groups: "Nobody was going to even consider splitting, so I backed off of that real fast."

Still, there is seductive appeal in the near-automatic growth implied in a plan that can be stated as follows: "Form group. Help that group grow to ten members. Split off new group. Repeat." We have told people, as we tried to persuade them to donate their apprentices and a few of their members to the seeding of a new group, that the process would ultimately be good for them. We've said things like this:

> We realize that it may be difficult for you, after being involved intimately with the lives and ideas of these particular people in your covenant group, but we ask you to think of this change as an opportunity to build relationships with new people and to provide new people the opportunity to develop relationships with you. Since the new covenant group members coming in will have different spiritual experiences and ideas, this will also provide you with the opportunity for more spiritual growth.

How many people do such arguments persuade? Almost none. Small Group Ministry seems to be a paradigm case of reality rudely failing to live up to theory.

Among those of us who believe that our nation would be a better place if there were more Unitarian Universalists than one in every one thousand or two thousand and that Small Group Ministry is an excellent way to reach out to the hundreds of folks in our neighborhoods who need liberal religion, the notion that covenant groups might help us begin to thrive through service is highly appealing. Images of statistical significance begin to dance in our heads, and we dream of societal influence rivaling the storied days of Ralph Waldo Emerson, Margaret Fuller, and Henry David Thoreau.

There is no doubt that small group organization can fuel remarkable growth in churches. Wuthnow, referring to Dr. Paul Cho's Full Gospel Yoido Church in Seoul, South Korea, says, "It grew to more than a half million members—all because of small groups." Wuthnow's research seems to have drawn him into contact with a lot of pastors who longed to soar to new professional heights by patterning their careers on one or another story of how small group organization can produce growth. Wuthnow writes,

> Every pastor seems to have a personal anecdote that proves the same point. The problem is an inversion of means and ends. What is the ultimate goal? Caring and supportive communities in which people can grow spiritually as they experience the love of others? Or a successful megachurch that boosts its image in the community and its pastor's salary at the same time? In some cases these two goals may work together, hand in hand. . . . But conflict between these two goals is also likely.

Wuthnow warns against undermining small groups in the pursuit of growth agendas. "Astute religious leaders," he says, "will recognize that small groups must be allowed to develop and mature at their own pace."

Groups do have stages of maturation and life cycles, Kennedy believes, and these need to be taken into consideration by facilitators and planners. Substituting the more generative term *birthing* for *splitting,* Kennedy said the following during the CCV Practitioners Summit discussion:

> In the initial stages, in the middle years, in the period of decline, there are really different dynamics going on. The receptivity of a group to birthing a new group, for example, may be very different depending on where the group is in its life cycle. If you push people to do something when the change you want is really not appropriate for the group at that time, you may have resistance that you wouldn't get at another time.

George, in *Prepare Your Church for the Future,* says the "gestation" period for healthy groups to grow and divide is two to twenty-four months. Thandeka urged practitioners to go easy on pushing for the spawning of new groups if covenant group members are resisting. "The rule is, you can't traumatize people," she said, and offered those attending the CCV Summit a theological basis for her view:

> From my standpoint, our spirituality, the mystical level of our religious movement, is based on a recognition that biology is first. Which is why we're not creedal. We should not put a creed, even one about size, ahead of affirming the worth and dignity of every individual and respecting the

bio-power of people being together. I think it would be a mistake for a group to go beyond a certain number. But if the group did go beyond that number, let the group gradually figure out what it's going to do, with the facilitator helping the process, so that the solution comes from the group.

Start, grow, divide? Send your apprentice and a few others off to start a new group once or twice a year? Wuthnow is on the side of those who resist. "Siphoning off every promising leader once every six months in order to start new groups," he says, "is certainly going to work against the functioning of the groups that already exist." It appears that the amoeba theory of small group growth has been done in by small group realities. So perhaps we should revert to George's position on the primacy of expert advice: Everyone working with meta-church groups should do things the way we say, unless they want to do them some other way. He also says, however, "If a group stays together for more than two years without becoming a parent, it stagnates."

Still, our desire to expand the number of covenant groups in our congregations was not driven entirely by a desire for numerical growth. At a General Assembly workshop in Salt Lake City, Dame spoke about his surprise at the degree to which his New England church, accustomed to the academic model of having the summer off from church life, had taken to Small Group Ministry:

I have come to deeply respect the need in our culture and our churches for a sense of intimacy and the opportunity to explore one's spiritual path. That is what these groups offer, and I have never encountered anything else in our church lives for which people would consider meeting every two weeks during the summer. I am very curious to see how this continues.

It isn't just ego gratification that draws many of us to be evangelical about Small Group Ministry. We want to serve the needs of more people and serve them better than we can without small group organization. But if our groups won't act like amoebas, how can we serve more and more of the individuals who need us? Some other approaches are being tried in our churches.

Offering Multiple Choices

At the CCV Practitioners Summit, after talking about how he backed off from the demand that groups split in the face of great resistance, McGee talked about his alternative strategies:

Now, what I'm doing is just giving groups a lot of options. We're having yearly re-evaluations of each group. We ask each group to take a look at what they want to do. Are they going to break up at that point? Are they going to continue? Are they going to help start another group, and, if so, is the apprentice going to facilitate that one? We offer all these possibilities for our groups while preaching the message of growth over and over again to the facilitators. There are lots of opportunities for people to get involved in various groups.

This approach results in groups reaching maximum size and ceasing to accept new members until a member leaves and opens a vacancy. People seeking covenant group membership, then, must be offered new groups. The church was adding a covenant group a month, at that time, so as noted earlier, McGee and his cominister, Gelbein, were busy finding and training facilitators.

New Groups for the New Folks

Dame's Augusta model also involves beginning new groups whenever there is sufficient demand and when Dame has found and trained a facilitator. Because all of that church's groups use Dame's session plans and none are formed around particular interests, outlooks, or activities, the main issue Dame has to work with in deciding where to place a new person, whether in a new group or an existing one with available space, is when the group meets. Members of the congregation showed no interest in what other congregations call *affinity groups* within the covenant group rubric (Christian groups, Buddhist groups, or gay/lesbian issue groups, for example). So, when needed, Dame told other practitioners at the Summit meeting, he and his folk start a new group: "We found only two sorting criteria which seemed to matter. The first was the night of the week, and the second was whether couples wanted to be in the same group or in different groups. Other than that, people just wanted a chance to be with other people and saw differences as attractive. We are talking about Unitarian Universalists, after all."

Oklahoma City's First Unitarian Universalist Church also starts new groups to meet growing need. Its covenant groups are affinity groups. When a covenant group with a particular focus has ten members and there are people who want to join, a new group with that focus is formed. A few months ago, the start of a Spiritual Growth Covenant Group was announced, and a sign-up sheet was posted. Response from the 350-member congregation exceeded expectations so much,

Mark Christian reported, that two more facilitators had to be found and trained so the church could launch three Spiritual Growth Covenant Groups at once.

The Unitarian Universalist Congregation of Binghamton, New York, began Small Group Ministry in October 2001, after a Turner workshop. The members were promised that there would be no pressure to divide groups for at least nine months. After seven covenant groups quickly formed, Whitney Herriage and lay leaders had a problem: It was hard to find enough facilitators. That, of course, is not the worst problem one can imagine.

Limited Time Expectations and Grace Periods

If covenant groups are, as Smith says, "a conversion experience," we may be wise to offer as many opportunities for covenant group experience as possible, even for limited times. Some evangelical Christian churches have short-term groups during which new folks may discover for themselves the benefits of small group organization without making lengthy commitments. One such congregation, discussed in Wuthnow's *I Came Away Stronger: How Small Groups Are Shaping American Religion,* has *First Groups* and *Home Fellowships.* People joining First Groups are expected to attend twelve weekly Bible study sessions that also encourage discussion of the previous Sunday's sermon. In this 3,000-member church that has 120 groups, First Group members have decisions to make at the end of their twelve weeks of meetings: "When a First Group completes its term, it may decide to extend its meetings, its participants may join a Home Fellowship, or its participants might be selected as candidates for leadership training with the goal that they will eventually start groups of their own." One couple, after their First Group experience, was chosen to form a new First Group. After three ninety-minute training sessions that included George's material, they were given about twenty names of prospective members, from which they collected a group of twelve active members that chose to stay together for twenty-five weeks.

Many of our congregations begin their covenant group programs as pilot projects that are expected to last six months or so, after which there is normally a process of evaluation that could lead to a full-scale program the following church year. Other congregations, while forming covenant groups as open-ended entities that may continue indefinitely, build in "grace periods," preannounced times (the month of May, perhaps) when anyone wishing to leave one covenant group and seek membership in another one or to cease covenant group participation altogether is encouraged to do so.

Although Robinson says it is his experience in the Brewster church that one covenant group in three will last ten years or more, some congregations are planning for much shorter terms. The Unitarian Universalist Congregation of Olympia, Washington, in its first year of a Small Group Ministry, expected each group to last only one year. Although this expectation could be one way of providing an annual entry time for new folks, Art Vaeni, the minister, observed that the motivation behind this "one-year, then re-group plan" is breadth of contact among church members:

> The main reason for doing this is that it will allow participants to develop deeper relationships with more members of the congregation over a period of several years. Conceivably, those who participate for five years could know as many as fifty people in the congregation quite intimately. What depth that would give to our understanding and feeling of community!

However, if we're to have short-term groups or times for members to leave, how should we note the ending of a group or the departure of a member of a group? Wuthnow's study of various kinds of small groups affiliated with religious organizations finds that groups with definite terms or checkpoints at which the group may decide to terminate or continue can use such occasions as times to celebrate accomplishments and say goodbye:

> What is more difficult, as we learned from talking with former members of some groups, is finding a way to celebrate with individual members who decide to terminate their participation. Those who move away are often given parties, whereas those who choose simply to drop out do so without fanfare, incurring guilt or resentment in the process. It is generally the responsibility of the group leader to seek them out and find a suitable way to commemorate their departure.

At a minimum, departing group members should be given extra time at their last meeting to reflect on their experience of the group, even if they found elements of that experience to be painful. Other group members, mindful of their shared-ministry roles, should offer the departing member appreciation for his or her positive contributions to the group. And when the group itself is ceasing to be, whether by preagreement or by a nonplanned decision of its members, the last meeting should be a celebration of all that was good about the group's life. If a covenant group holds only three meetings and serves only five people before folding, we should honor the fact that five people got a taste of covenant group experience, got to know each other somewhat better, and learned a little or a lot. It is better to publish an announcement in the church newsletter of the group's ending, with thanks to leaders and participants, than to let a group's ending, planned or not, go unmarked.

Is It Easier for the Young to Split?

Michelle Bohls of First Unitarian Universalist Church in Austin, Texas, says that the church's "first official covenant group" of young adults had decided, on the first anniversary of its formation, to birth a second group. Bohls is a key lay leader of the church's two hundred-member VOYAGers organization for people in their twenties and thirties. After a year of having one covenant group, splitting off a second, and seeing how that worked, Bohls wrote, "We're committed to the covenant group format and began to recognize how not doing what the model says to do can hurt the group dynamics. I feel hopeful that these two new groups will be four new groups a year from now."

The *Child Group* welcomes people new to the church and to VOYAGers. These folks and their mother group have cooperated on fund-raising projects, and Bohls was pleased by the ease with which newer covenant group members were able fit in at a forty-member VOYAGer retreat. She counts that as the most encouraging sign of the split-off group's success. "Because these newer people had a base of friendships started in their covenant group," she says, "they felt like part of the community already and were able to successfully assimilate into the larger group."

While this success story of a mother group giving birth to a child group might lead one to believe that younger people find splitting groups to be easier to accomplish than older people do, Bohls says it has not been entirely easy: "It's been a challenge as each group needs to be nurtured and guided. People seem to just naturally want to resist the rules, to tweak them. The rewards of doing it according to plan, though, are well worth it and I see that once people 'get it,' the covenant group approach can transform lives and our community."

Different Solutions for Different Models

During the CCV Practitioners Summit discussion on starting new groups, Kennedy speculated that the issue may vary depending on whether a congregation is offering minister-guided, spiritual development groups, such as in Augusta, Maine, or theme groups, like those in Brewster, Massachusetts, and the congregation where she was then working as a religious educator, All Souls in Kansas City, Missouri. There will be more natural attrition in some groups focused on a theme, a topic, or an activity, she said, citing as an example a covenant group for parents of teenagers. As birthdays come and go, some parents get beyond the need for the group's sharing of problems and successes with rearing teens, and therefore spaces open up. "I don't think the problem of how to get new groups going is as difficult if you have theme groups as opposed to having generic spiritual development groups," Kennedy said, "so the problem looks different depending on the model you're using."

The Varieties of Small Group Experience

Poor Adam! During the first few days of his existence, the Bible says, he was asked to name all the other living things God was creating. That could not have been easy work, with God turning out creature after creature, and Adam came up with some names he must have regretted as soon as Cain and Abel got old enough to raise questions. Imagine being asked, "Dad, how did you come up with *aardvark?*"

Early promoters of the grassroots movement for small group organization can sympathize with Adam's plight. Tuner began with the term *meta-church groups,* which others found to be about as elegant as *orangutan.* When thirty or more leadership school participants were asked to help come up with a name for these groups of ten, they produced many suggestions, no one of which was liked by more than two or three in the group. *Covenant groups* grew out of that exercise. Dame and his congregation came up with *Small Group Ministry,* and others prefer *Covenant Group Ministry.* Each term has detractors, and the titles churches have given to their own versions of Small Group Ministry are about as varied as the fishes of the sea or the birds of the air.

After naming comes taxonomy. Classification has its own pitfalls. Given Adam's mixed success with naming, God may have awarded Eve the task of sorting creatures into groups and labeling each one. The Bible seems to be silent on this point, but if Eve was the taxonomist, she did some good work. *Monopod,* for example, makes sense. But why did she list the garden-variety tomato as a fruit?

Any taxonomy of Small Group Ministries, of course, will be just as open to question. Nevertheless, within the realm of creation known as Unitarian Universalism, Small Group Ministries thus far may be said to have produced four definable types: curriculum-directed, minister-directed, theology-directed, and interest-directed.

Curriculum-Directed Small Group Ministries

Smith developed an adaptation of meta-church technique during the 1990s while he was senior minister at All Souls in Tulsa, Oklahoma. He called his program Roots and Branches, and at least one of our congregations is using a successful adaptation of this approach.

The Roots part, as Smith defined it, was for people considering membership in the church. It consisted of four sessions of adult education classes taught by the ministers of the church and focusing on the history and heritage of both Unitarian Universalism and All Souls. Graduates of those sessions were offered the opportunity to join the church and/or to become members of *Branches Groups* of up to twelve persons plus a lay leader, meeting once or twice a month.

Smith provided study material on twelve topics in a manual entitled *Branches, Part One: The Free Church Tradition.* In it he described the intent of the overall program:

> In sessions with a trained leader, you will learn about the difference between orthodox and liberal religion, the concepts of the free pulpit and the free pew, separation of church and state, and the idea of "covenant" which is a stronger connection amongst people than common belief. You will learn how old the radical idea of the complete freedom and full dignity of an individual is. . . . Finally, you will learn how freedom encourages all people to think reasonably, and to use all reasonable resources and means to live their lives.

An accompanying leader's guide included four session outlines, some opening and closing readings, and a section on philosophy and implementation. In that document, Smith cited two "unbreakable rules of Branches small group study": "First, . . . each Branches Group must relate itself intentionally to the larger church community in which it is located. . . . Secondly, each Branches Group must replicate itself; that is, birth a separate group." Smith saw his role, as senior minister, to be one of "casting the vision," or reasserting the church's goals and purpose. He saw the role of the covenant groups as being the extension of that vision out into the community in ever-widening circles.

The emphasis on learning or, from the leaders' viewpoints, on teaching, distinguishes this model from the others. Having as its foundation a set of written materials on Unitarian Universalist history and heritage, the Roots and Branches model is curriculum based, and the minister has primary responsibility as lead teacher. Although Smith's approach was more didactic than the others, it did give people ways to build relationships with one another. A member, who told Smith she had left All Souls in the 1980s in order to find companionship in another congregation, returned and stayed because of Roots and Branches. Another person told Smith that being in a Small Group Ministry was "the most important thing that has ever happened to me in my life. I've discovered lifelong friendships here, people I will grow old with."

In 1997, some of Smith's materials were adapted for use in starting a covenant group for members of the Northwest Community Unitarian Universalist Church of Houston. Before the first session was over, it was clear that the people attending that start-up covenant group had less interest in history and heritage than in sharing reflections and stories from their own lives. The focus soon shifted to discussion of books suggested by members, and the group continues and now calls itself The Salon.

For the last couple of years, our Baton Rouge, Louisiana, congregation has been using its own adaptation of the Roots and Branches materials under the leadership of Steve Crump. A primer published by the church for the groups suggests two purposes for the Roots section: Participants will become better acquainted with Crump though his teaching of the Roots material, and they will learn about liberal religious traditions. As at All Souls Church in Tulsa, Roots classes are a prerequisite for Branches Groups.

The Baton Rouge version of Roots and Branches differs, though, in some significant ways. One is that long-term church members, in addition to new members, those considering membership, and visitors, are welcome to attend Roots classes in Baton Rouge. A second difference is in the session material for Branches Groups. Bob and Diana Dorroh, facilitators of the church's first Branches Group, found that the Tulsa-church material worked for them, but other groups wanted something different. As a result, Branches facilitators turned to *Transforming Your*

Churches with Small Group Ministry, the work of Turner, one of their church's former ministers.

For a time, it appeared that this program was having little effect on membership. During the third year of the Roots and Branches program, however, Diana Dorroh reported a 50-member increase from a year earlier, to 350 adults. Attendance at two Sunday services was up as well. The Southwest District's growth consultant, Jonalu Johnstone, in a report sent to church leaders after a visit in June 2002, says that this "appears to be a thriving, growing church," with Branches Groups serving about one-third of the membership.

Having expressed the opinion some months earlier that Small Group Ministry in Baton Rouge needed a staff person in addition to the senior minister for best functioning, Diana Dorroh began filling that role as a volunteer. She says her aspiration, though, "is to be replaced by a paid staff person or a second minister on staff."

Minister-Directed Small Group Ministries

Small Group Ministry began at the Unitarian Universalist Community Church of Augusta, Maine, in April 1999, when the church had about 165 members, the same number it had claimed for several years. Since then, Dame says, the church has had an increase of more than 35 members, with as many as half in covenant groups at any given time. Accompanying this gain was a 26 percent increase in money raised through the church's annual canvass one year, and the congregation has succeeded in financing a building program. Such progress, Dame says, would not have happened without Small Group Ministry, which "invites lay people to enter into a different relationship with each other and it teaches that the outcome of a spiritual life is ministry, is service."

Two distinguishing characteristics of the successful program at the Unitarian Universalist Community Church in Augusta are these:

- The minister has primary responsibility for providing session plans.
- The minister assigns people to the groups.

In what some people may consider to be a fine example of understatement, Dame says, "All in all, the program we envisioned calls for more ministerial authority than Unitarian Universalists are usually comfortable with." It was, however, a program lay folk in Augusta wanted. Dame observes,

The meta-church material that we studied comes from a tradition which is much more hierarchical than most Unitarian Universalist congregations. As we considered how the program might work, and what we wanted to accomplish, we discussed the balance of authority and autonomy in the life of our congregation, and the strength and weaknesses of different arrangements.

The result is a unique approach that, as Dame notes, has worked quite well so far.

Dame chooses, trains, and meets regularly with facilitators. Sometimes he attends covenant group meetings to assist facilitators with difficulties, and, he says, he is the chief cheerleader and vision caster: "Through the newsletter and from the pulpit, by recognition and encouragement, I keep people in mind of the fact that we are all called to ministry, that the small groups have revitalized the life of the congregation, that there is always room for new participants, and that the work of the small groups is the work of the church." The church has an ongoing steering committee that works with Dame to sort out problems, to look ahead, and to plan for change.

Although the church's lay leaders deemed Dame's session plan writing and new member assignment duties important enough to get priority over other tasks normally seen as being the minister's responsibility, they now have given him help in both areas. When requests for additional session plans grew beyond Dame's ability to turn them out, the Small Group Ministry Steering Committee appointed a topics subcommittee. This group, working with the minister, generates ideas, writes first drafts, edits them, and when there is consensus that they are ready, adds them to the growing collection of approved materials.

Facilitators, who are assured that they don't have to be experts on any evening's topic, are given session plan notebooks. Each plan is built around questions intended to encourage deep reflection and conversation on topics such as worship, loneliness, loss, idealism, transcendence, sin, prayer, fear, and healing. Although groups may choose, for any of their meetings, any one of the more than one hundred approved session plans, when groups take up session plans that they know others are using also, "the sense of connection is deepened and strengthened," Dame says.

In many congregations, people choose to join groups that are going to be focusing on particular topics or activities, but because the Augusta Unitarian Universalist Community Church has no interest-focused groups, it needed another means of forming Small Group Ministries. Its solution: Let the minister, taking into consideration the times when people are available and anything else he may know about them, assign people to groups. Recognizing that not all the matches will work out, though, the church's Small Group Ministry Steering Committee instituted a "re-up day," a day, announced in advance, when people could freely leave a group and seek another one. As the church approached its first re-up day, only two people out of ninety covenant group participants indicated interest in changing groups. Even these two changed their minds and stayed with their assigned groups in the end.

In the third year of its Small Group Ministry program, the congregation provided Dame some help by hiring a part-time Small Group Ministry coordinator. This coordinator keeps track of which groups have spaces available for new members; talks with people interested in joining groups; consults with the minister about placements; and to stay in touch with covenant group events, attends facilitator meetings. Dame said recently,

> With nearly as many adults in Small Group Ministry as children in Religious Education, we realized that this vital program would require similar resources. Our success lies in part in the commitment of the whole congregation to a different paradigm of congregational life, and the realization that it takes a commitment of resources to keep our small groups healthy— the minister's time, laypeople's time, and money.

Having emphasized communication at the start of their program, the leaders of this church continue to do so by putting articles in each newsletter, publishing brochures, and mentioning Small Groups Ministry in both welcome letters sent to newcomers and oral welcomes during Sunday services. Once or twice a year, the sermon is related to covenant groups, and facilitators are frequently recognized and thanked for the ministry they provide. Each new person who joins a group is given a handbook that describes the program and the way it works.

The ministry staff of one of our largest congregations, in Arlington, Virginia, has provided materials to covenant group sessions in a different way: through sermons. During this congregation's 2000–2001 church year, for example, fifteen covenant groups with an average attendance of about eight people met monthly to consider topics provided by a sermon series entitled "Are the Big Questions Multiple Choice?" The ministry team of McGee and Gelbein preached on major questions of life today, and the church's other team member, Linda Olson Peebles, led children in a monthly service on the same topics. (Ten other covenant groups in the church continued with the topics of activities around which they'd been formed.)

McGee found that this way of providing material for Small Group Ministries worked well in the subsequent church year, an especially difficult one for a congregation located only a few miles from the Pentagon in Washington, D.C., the site of one of the September 11, 2001, terrorist attacks:

> I was thrilled that we involved the entire congregation, all ages and philosophies, in conversing with each other about some of the most significant questions: What is the meaning of life? Why do we need religion? Why evil? How do we know what we know? How can we face death? Why do we suffer? What does it mean to be human? How can we survive? We had planned this program long before September 11th, but I can think of no better way for us to have ministered to each than to have these sermons and covenant groups available to our members and friends. They gave people the chance not only to ask the big questions that were so prominent in everyone's minds, but to have others genuinely listen, respond, and share feelings and ideas.

The ministry team's theme for the 2002–2003 church year sought to build on the success of the "big questions" series. "The Challenge of Religious Pluralism: Searching for the Big Answers" was the follow-up title, and again, children in religious education classes and those covenant groups that chose to focused on the answers proclaimed by the religions of the world.

"Spiritual intimacy," in the view of Laurel Hallman, senior minister of another of our largest congregations, First Unitarian Church of Dallas, "is an important quality of highly functioning covenant groups." Hallman's video entitled *Living by Heart* is about spirituality, and her influence can be seen in the opening and closing questions normally used for that church's Deepening Groups. They often begin with the question, How is your spirit this evening? The standard closing question is, What would you like us to carry in our thoughts and prayers until our next meeting?

It is the Deepening Group facilitators, working with Susan Madison, director of adult education, however, who are responsible for choosing the questions to be used by groups at First Unitarian Church of Dallas groups. The facilitators are compiling a file of session materials to share with one another. Some questions used for discussion starters recently have included the following:

- What is an example of grace in your life?
- When have you experienced a heartfelt truth, and how did it change your life?
- What about your daily work do you find nourishing?

Theology-Directed Small Group Ministries

At the heart of theology-directed model is a particular understanding of religion and the sources of covenant group power, along with an emphasis on service to the larger community. Thandeka, associate professor of theology and culture at Meadville/Lombard Theological School, Chicago, is the founder of the Center for Community Values, whose purpose is the promotion of small group organization in Unitarian Universalist congregations and beyond.

Although the covenant group approach advocated by the CCV follows the fundamental patterns of small group organization, Thandeka believes that additional elements are necessary. Covenant groups, she says, "heal and repair the human heart; they heal and repair the world." To further that healing and "to experientially affirm the members' spiritual life as part of a beloved community," Thandeka recommends that covenant group facilitators begin with brief exercises designed to focus attention on the present moment, the here-and-now reality of existence. The CCV's *Sourcebook* says:

> The opening ritual marks the beginning of the group's time together. This ritual ties the group to the larger organization of which it is a part and reminds the group of its transcendent purpose. Ritual exemplifies an embodied spirituality. It is a time for centering and for helping the members make the transition from the busy-ness of daily life to the more intentional and focused activity and discussion of the group.

This centering time can include a song, a reading, a prayer, the lighting of a chalice or candle, or other rituals that "help the members to relax, center, breathe a little deeper and let go of the mundane thoughts with which they have entered the meeting." Here are some elements of covenant group openings Thandeka recommends in the CCV *Sourcebook,*

> The members of the group simply sit quietly and listen to the sounds in the room, focus steady attention on an object, pay attention to the rise and fall of their own breath, or practice other forms of concentration that tend to relax their bodies and quiet their minds so that they can be fully present to and with each other. Then, each person has the opportunity to talk about what's going on in her or his life.

For the end of the meeting, she recommends a similar closing ritual: "Each meeting ends as it began, with a ritual that re-affirms the embodied feelings of the group for each member of the group." These rituals in Small Group Ministry "embrace our humanity and in this embrace restore our humanity."

Covenant groups, Thandeka believes, are "sacramental acts of right relationship" that have redemptive power. The healing power that she finds integral to covenant group effectiveness in human lives, she said in an address at Unity Church, Unitarian, in St. Paul, Minnesota, has been called by many names:

> With Henry Nelson Wieman we call it "creative interchange." With James Luther Adams, we call it "community creating power." With Margaret Fuller, we call it "dwelling in the ineffable, the unutterable"—dwelling within "God." With Martin Buber we feel it in the space created between you and me, I and Thou, and we call it "the Eternal Thou."

This collective power, created when individuals gather as a religious community, Thandeka says, is the fundamental source of Unitarian Universalist authority. In covenant groups, "We know it as the healing and transformational power of life itself. We are transformed by this act into a religious people."

A part of that healing, in the CCV approach, occurs through community activism. From the beginning of this grassroots movement in Unitarian Universalism, the atmosphere of trust generated in covenant groups has held out promise of allowing us to face more successfully the many difficult issues of social and cultural change that demand our attention. The overflow of goodwill that can come from a covenant group's shared experience of compassion and well-being, Thandeka says in the *Sourcebook,* "gives some participants the collective ability to participate in community outreach projects that transport the covenant group beyond itself."

As we noted earlier, the experiences of McGee and Robinson support Thandeka's view. After working together in community projects, McGee's covenant group members "come back jazzed," and social justice work by small groups in Robinson's church has earned it a reputation for caring and effectiveness.

Interest-Directed Small Group Ministries

In discussions of Small Group Ministry, *affinity groups* is the term most often used for groups gathered around the particular interests of individual members.

Covenant groups might form around shared interests in existentialist philosophy, creative writing, hiking, quilting, parenting, investing, particular religious outlooks, and the improvement of the lives of mothers on welfare. These topics and scores of other topics and activities have drawn people together into Small Group Ministries.

Prominent among our congregations using the affinity model of Small Group Ministry is the Brewster congregation. Some of that church's groups follow the Small Group Ministry model, and some don't. Robinson recalls that when he and other church leaders were planning the church's transition some years ago from midsize to large, they needed ways to help people grieve for the changes the church was going through because of growth. They offered a list of forty possible groups and asked members to indicate which ones drew their interest. Then they sought good facilitators for those groups that drew the most interest. The result, Robinson said during a gathering of covenant group practitioners a couple of years ago, was "a geometric expansion of small groups. Maybe twenty-five or thirty actually took off." They included a single-parent group, a couples group, a gay group, a lesbian group, a Christian group, a Buddhist group, and many others.

Robinson's view of Small Group Ministry is very much in line with that of other practitioners of small group organization. He said at the Practitioners' Summit,

> To my way of looking at it, Small Group Ministry has a spiritual core. The whole group and the individual are contained in some larger presence than human will power and everybody knows it. The second component is authentic community where people can show up and feel "I am valued for being me, for being what I am. I will listen well to the other person." So community, intimate community, is being created. The third component is that every group needs to do service. People stay around when they feel like they're giving something. Almost all of our groups would say "We are serving the world by being a small group."

Although Robinson and his staff choose facilitators carefully, train them, and assist with covenant group formation, they don't attempt to direct the focus of the groups that form. An assumption that underlies the affinity groups model of Small Group Ministry is that virtually any activity or shared interest brought to the covenant group format can facilitate openness and interaction. Some people will be drawn to curriculum-based groups that begin with history and heritage. Some will be eager to join ministry-focused groups discussing grief, joy, and other topics.

Some will be especially interested in theologically grounded groups that can help them get in touch with their bodies as a means of opening the heart and mind. Others may prefer different paths toward the same ends. Robinson says,

> We have retired humanists who wouldn't go near a touchy-feely topic in a hundred years. They have the most vigorous discussions on the human condition and they come alive. The drummers don't want to talk; they drum. It depends on the group's spirituality. Goddess groups will dance. The humanists will check in, but they won't call it "check in."

At our General Assembly in 2002, a woman attending a workshop asked for help in attracting men to her congregation's covenant group program, which, she said, is composed almost entirely of women. At the time of the CCV Practitioners Summit, Robinson's church had five groups specifically for men, having begun with one and expanded as the need arose. Some men may be more likely to open up while swinging a hammer on a Habitat for Humanity construction site than in a circle in a living room. But shared activity can be a stimulus for verbal exchange for women, too. For hundreds of years many women , busily pushing needles through cloth, have experienced a rich flow of conversation around a quilting frame.

An affinity covenant group meeting, having begun with an opening reading, a ritual, or both and having attended to what each person has brought to check-in, may focus on any topic or activity appropriate for adult religious liberals who are members of a particular congregation within the Unitarian Universalist Association, and the result will be Small Group Ministry. One of the covenant groups formed by the Unitarian Universalist Fellowship in the Oak Cliff section of Dallas is for single, widowed, or divorced members of the church. Their ritual involves meeting at someone's home, beginning with a Unitarian Universalist reading, and checking in. Then they all go out to dinner together.

Covenant groups give us a way of structuring our interactions so that all of us, the quiet ones as well as the verbally quick, may be heard and made to feel a part of the whole. Any viable form of small group organization that produces mutual trust and service to others is a benefit to our faith. In the future we may discover that there are more than these four models of Small Group Ministry experience.

A New Model of Ministry

The premise of Small Group Ministry is that we all share in the ministry of our congregations. Still, there are issues of particular significance for professional, called ministers, and this chapter may be of more interest to them than to lay leaders. Small Group Ministry changes the way our churches are organized and, for most of us, the way we think about Unitarian Universalist ministry. Why would anybody suggest such a thing? Ministers hardly have time to think, be with family and friends, tend to self-care, or deepen our spiritual lives. One can almost hear the mental objections: "With so much wood to cut and so little time, how can anyone suggest that I try another kind of saw? I don't even have time to sharpen the one I got from my mentors. Go away! I'm busy sawing."

Unfortunately for anyone feeling this way, even if all the proponents of this change do go away, it's too late. Small Group Ministry is out of the bag, and too many people in too many churches already love it. It's time to consider changing saws. A primary reason is succinctly noted in a *Journal of Liberal Religion* article by an associate professor of ministry at Meadville Lombard Theological School, David Bumbaugh. Noting that the number of Unitarian Universalists in the world today is not as large as it was at the time of consolidation in 1961, Bumbaugh writes,

Whatever you make of these numbers, one fact remains indisputable. Every year since merger, Unitarian Universalism has lost market share. Our growth has never matched the rate of the growth of the nation's population as a whole.

Market share? Who cares? We should. To say we have lost "market share" is to say that we have been slipping in our ability to serve the people in our communities who need us. Paul Ray assures us that there are plenty of them, but for the past four decades, the portion we have been able to serve has declined. Most of our congregations draw in as many visitors every year as they have members, or more, but only a handful stay to join. Does this mean we should keep doing what we have been doing?

A second reason for moving toward small group organization has to do with the mental, emotional, and physical health of the minister. None of our churches, regardless of size, can pay for all the ministry their members need. Ministers serving our congregations—large, midsize, and small—have to deal constantly with the draining awareness that they do not have enough time or energy to respond positively to all the needs of their parishioners. The "saw" we've been using is burning out our best, most caring ministers. Change is frightening, but so are the panic and despair one sees in the eyes of our parish ministers, especially in the late spring, when the fresh promise of the new church year is just a distant memory but vacation is still several Sundays (that is, several sermons and at least a few crises) away. We can't afford not to find a new model of ministry.

There is significant help in the shared ministry that can bloom in facilitated groups of up to ten church members. Small Group Ministry can leverage the work of the congregation's called minister. The anticipated gains are both self-focused and altruistic. Ministers can feel better about themselves as agents of increased success in meeting their churches' needs, and those churches can be revived through serving better than ever before the thousands in all our communities who need liberal religion. Perhaps we Unitarian Universalists can even become a significant force for good in the world again.

It's quite a vision. So why haven't we done it already? Why did we miss the power of small group organization for so many years when other church groups were flourishing through its use? Why might we continue to miss it now? We may have to look to ourselves for the answers. Our own attitudes and beliefs could be holding us back.

"I'm Tough"

Good ole boy, a female colleague said recently, is not a gender-specific label. The influx of women into our ministry has brought a diminishment of the peacock-like strutting one-upsmanship that once characterized ministers' gatherings, and the machismo of good-ole-boy ministry has faded. Today's ministers' meetings, however, sometimes display a different sort of competitiveness and assertion of personal importance. Colleagues at today's ministers' meetings tend to say things like: "You think you're busy and overworked. Well, let me tell you about busy!" Like people in other professions in today's world, we seem to think that if we're insanely preoccupied with work, we must be important.

Not that shifting to Small Group Ministry, in the beginning at least, will free up lots of time and energy for things like spiritual exploration and personal growth. Charles Gaines, writing in 1999 for *Covenant Group News* about his first experience serving a congregation that was trying out a small group approach, confesses his surprise at the success and effectiveness of those small groups. "Three years ago, I never would have believed all this could happen," he says, adding, "after forty years in ministry, I have not experienced anything quite like this." Success, though, did come at a cost. Gaines also writes, "When this began I did not realize how time-consuming it would be. The time I've given this program prevented me from doing other things. I believe it was time well spent, but anyone who wishes to duplicate this idea needs to realize that it demands a lot of a minister's time."

At the CCV Facilitators Summit, Jane Bramadat spoke of sometimes feeling overwhelmed by the extra workload that Small Group Ministry brought to her professional life as an interim minister, and McGee said he'd felt that, too. But there is a way out of this dilemma. Sharing ministry includes sharing burdens. McGee went to his covenant group leaders for help with his feeling of being overwhelmed, and he and his lay folk began figuring out ways to spread the load more evenly.

Then, however, McGee found within himself an attitude that could have derailed the help that was available to him because of Small Group Ministry. He found that he did not entirely want help. He said, "This program was taking more and more of my time and energy. The thing was, I was really enjoying doing this. So part of me hated to give it up, while another part of me was saying, 'Hey, I just can't do this by myself.'"

Phyllis L. Hubbell and John Manwell of First Unitarian Church, Baltimore, cofacilitated one of their congregation's early covenant groups. Then they pulled back so they'd have more time to anchor the facilitators' covenant group and to allow a lay facilitator to step forward. Giving up being covenant group facilitators, though, was not easy. Facilitating covenant groups, Hubbell says, "feeds us ministers as much as our church members."

"But I'm the Minister"

A second source of excessive stoicism for ministers may be a variation on "That's just how we do things around here." Early imprinting tells most of us that to be a minister is to be very like the first minister we knew well and admired. He or she didn't complain, at least not aloud to us. Perhaps that minister was present and crucially important when there was a death in the family or she helped us celebrate a marriage. Male or female, these minister models had no need, so far as we knew, of a cadre of lay ministers. For most of us, ministry is what they did, plus the improvements we've brought to their techniques.

John Morgan, writing for *Covenant Group News* in March 2000, says, "Small Group Ministry will change the very nature of our churches and the leadership which guides them. One minister simply cannot be 'in charge' of a church which adopts a Small Group Ministry. It takes a different model of ministry—shared ministry—to work."

Russell Lockwood, mentor to many ministers serving our churches today, often offered advice that came down to this: "If you need to be out in front leading the parade, find something else to do. When we do our work well in a church other people will think what happened was their idea." Shared ministry requires us to yield some of the limelight and some of the power to which most of us are accustomed. "Some ministers," Morgan says, "still want to hold onto the authority." George agrees, noting the needs of some ministers "to be right and to be in control, lest their competence seem challenged or threatened." He writes in *Prepare Your Church for the Future,*

> This kind of minister will experience difficulty in multiplying teachers, advisors, counselors, and other persons of wisdom, since these lay pastors may come to wield almost as much influence in their small groups as their senior pastor. Similarly, some pastors become wounded or jealous when their lay ministers receive the affirmation that used to be reserved for the professional minister.

There can be more at stake here than the sharing of affirmation of course. George notes that ministers can usually relate stories of at least one small group that "became a power center of gossip and divisive discussion." Every parish has at least one, two, or a few folks who are unhappy with our ministries. Unhappy parishioners are often eager to find forums in which to seek allies, so any minister might be tempted to prohibit covenant groups from forming around political or divisive issues within the church. Covenant groups are intended to provide opportunities for building mutual trust and to help lift members' outlooks from the mundane to higher levels of purpose and commitment. Divisiveness works against both those goals.

Despite these risks, however, George sees the gains of Small Group Ministry as far outnumbering the losses if ministers "properly manage their groups through monitoring, teaching, and providing curriculum resources." Diana Dorroh, a covenant group facilitator in Baton Rouge, has been in two Branches Groups that had discussions of divisive church issues, and results in both cases were positive. She says, "I see our groups offering reassurance to members who are worried about the effects of church conflicts, to put it all in perspective, and to let our newer members realize that problems are nothing new, but are just part of being a community. It would feel very strange to have to avoid church issues."

Dorroh notes that there are a couple of built-in safeguards against possible difficulties. One is that the covenants of each group should serve as a curb on argumentation and politicking. And the other safeguard is that the minister chooses facilitators and meets with them regularly. Divisiveness is something facilitators should work to diminish in covenant group discussions, whether the topic is the attainment of nirvana or the minister's reluctance to go to two services each Sunday.

Hard to Give Up

Even Calvin Dame, one of the earliest and most enthusiastic advocates of Small Group Ministry, had difficulty in accepting fully the change that small group organization brought to the way he was expected to do ministry in our Augusta church. He tells of the day he learned about the death of a member's father, not from the grieving young woman but from a member of her covenant group, and two months (two months!) after the event. "Don't worry," his informant said, "she's doing fine. We took care of her." Dame was glad, of course, to know that she had been taken care of, but he found that he had to deal with a number of feelings of his own. In his *Small Group Ministry Resource Book,* he says, "First, I felt inadequate. How come I did not know about this? Did they assume I didn't care? Then I was annoyed. Why did no one let me know? Then I was hurt. I wanted to be the one who was there for her! I wanted to be the minister!"

Finally, Dame worked his way to "grudging appreciation." The shared ministry of the church had held the woman in tender care when she needed just that. Dame concludes, "The ministry of our congregation goes on in circles beyond my participation, beyond the limitations of my time and attention. That this is so is a circumstance to be welcomed, cherished, and celebrated." Still, Dame had some grieving to do, and during the CCV Practitioners Summit, he explained the source of that grief:

> Many of us were called to the ministry because we wanted to help, we wanted to be part of people's lives. We like being up there on Sunday mornings and we like hearing people say, a few months after they've been through something traumatic, "I'm so glad you were there for me. It was so important that you were there for me at that time." We want those goodies. We not only want to do that sort of one-to-one care, we want what comes back to us after we've done it.

How many parishioners can one professional minister serve adequately? The estimates vary. I've assumed the number was between 100 and 125 adults. Dame has said "no more than 125 to 140, tops. The single-minister model can't move beyond that. It's just not going to work." Could there be a relationship between this upper limit and the fact that our average congregation has fewer than 150 members? Could we, as ministers, have unwittingly made sure that our flocks did not get too large for the shepherd? Or have the circumstances of traditional, ordinary ministry contained inherent, self-limiting effects resulting in small congregations that take in only enough members to replace those who die or move?

Serving Whose Needs?

In any case, the idea that a single minister can serve even an average-size Unitarian Universalist congregation, using the methods common to the current and previous generations of clergy, may be optimistic. In *Prepare Your Church for the Future*, George asks whether a pastor or skilled lay leader can care adequately for a group even as small as fifty to one hundred and offers a firm opinion: "In reality, he or she cannot. What actually transpires is a limited intimacy and a limited accountability. Over time, many people grow dissatisfied and disillusioned, not understanding why it's so hard to go deeper in feelings of caring and belonging."

Traditionally organized churches are not prepared to deal with the needs of the people coming through their doors, George says. With evident exasperation, he asks, "What makes pastors and lay leaders dare to imagine that the existing forum of congregation-size gatherings allows for quality caring? Our traditional way of viewing what ministry is has blinded us to the needs of the people God sends our way." The idea that a minister can meet the needs of up to one hundred people in the "do it yourself concept of parish ministry," he says, must give way to the vision of each minister working with lay ministers caring for groups of ten.

Ah, but George is talking about Christian congregations. Perhaps we Unitarian Universalists are different. Probably not. Our congregations too often have been characterized by "limited intimacy and a limited accountability," resulting in our shrugging our shoulders and accepting what we know as the norm, just the way things go. We all know of people who have left our churches because of a perceived lack of depth in caring and belonging. Most of our ministers stay, continuing to serve as ministers, and not only because of the pay. As Dame recognizes, most get a lot of inner reward from being ministers. Could it be that traditionally organized churches serve the needs of our ministers better than they serve the needs of most of our parishioners?

Answers to one of the questions in the Fulfilling the Promise survey reported to the General Assembly in 2000 may speak to this question. Because about ten thousand people responded—close to one in every fifteen of us—this survey provides a remarkable window into some aspects of who we Unitarian Universalists are. But before we look at one of its questions, please consider whether you agree that a central reason for the existence of any Unitarian Universalist congregation is this: to be an outlet for one's deepest understandings of life in the midst of a community of faith, experience, and spiritual growth. Agreed? The answers produced by this survey suggest that our churches are such an outlet for some of us, but significantly less so for others.

What would be missing in your life, one survey question asked, if Unitarian Universalism ceased being available? Half of the ministers who responded, 50 percent, chose the following answer "An outlet for my deepest understanding in a community of faith, experience, and spiritual growth." Only 30 percent of lay folk who responded to the survey, members of our churches all, chose that answer; 70 percent did not. If the covenant group movement excites lay people more than it excites ministers initially, as it did in Dame's church and it does in many other congregations, is that because half our ministers, but less than a third of our lay people, have been finding their traditionally organized churches to be outlets for their "deepest understanding in a community of faith, experience, and spiritual growth"? Was the old way of organizing our churches serving ministers better than lay people?

Dame thinks there is another reason why ministers may have been slower than some lay folk to pick up on the benefits of small group organization: Many ministers already were experiencing the benefits covenant groups bring to lay folk. During the CCV Practitioners Summit, he said,

> What people get out of Small Group Ministry, ministers get out of their professional groups when they work well, and in the Northeast we have a great professional group. We'd drive four hours through a snowstorm to sit in a room with our peers. It was a place where we could say, "The people in my church are driving me crazy!" And everybody says, "Oh yeah, I know what you mean," because they do know what you mean. So I wasn't feeling a lack of that in my life. But people in the congregation got a glimpse of this as a possibility: a place to sit down, share these important parts of their lives. That was powerful enough for the people in my congregation to pull me along and lead me to change.

Much of the success of this movement thus far, Dame believes, is due to the extent to which it has been a grassroots, collaborative process, often with lay folk leading the way.

During the summit discussions, Kennedy, speaking as a ministerial student, expressed the optimistic view that the upcoming generation of ministers may have fewer difficulties than their predecessors with shared ministry:

> When I think about my colleagues at Meadville/Lombard, the other students, I would say they are ready for this already. They're not thinking they need to be the minister in control. They're wanting to approach ministry collaboratively and they're ready for tools to allow that. They might be more receptive than we think.

Such a generation-based shift could be lucky for us and for them if Wuthnow is right when he says that "the sacred is being redefined, turned on its authoritarian head, made more populist, practical, and experiential." The small group movement "focuses members' attention on each others' needs and on helping people they know personally," he says, and it is succeeding in this country "because it encourages grass-roots participation." In what could be seen as a restatement of the purpose of Small Group Ministry, George says in *The Coming Church Revolution* that the goal of any effective organizational system is "to assure the highest level of care at the lowest level in the structure." Small Group Ministry moves to a lower level of our church structures (the facilitated group of ten or fewer) a higher level of care (shared ministry).

Retire the old saws. The new ones are sharp.

Current Issues, Future Directions

Many who believe in Small Group Ministry were surprised and pleased at the number of ministers who pushed back their chairs and stood during a luncheon at a Unitarian Universalist ministers' convocation in 2002. They'd been asked to stand if they were serving churches with covenant group programs in place. In that dining hall for the 450-minister gathering, according to the estimates of two independent observers, at least 70 percent stood. One observer thought it was 80 percent. It would have been wonderful to see even half of the ministers on their feet, especially because some of those present were community ministers not serving churches directly. It was enough to tempt one to mix metaphors and declare, This grassroots movement has taken flight

Small Group Ministry, riding the small group wave Wuthnow has documented in our larger society, has spread rapidly through our churches and fellowships. We're making great time, but where are we going? The fact that we didn't know how many of our congregations are using Small Group Ministry illustrates our lack of hard data. Only a couple of studies exist to go along with the wealth of stories we have generated about this movement, which is only about halfway through its first decade. What we do know, though, suggests a few persistent problems, some interesting trends, and a few possibilities for exploration. If we are able to solve our problems satisfactorily, where will Small Group Ministry be in, say, 2010?

Although one study we do have in hand focused on a single congregation, it produced results that are compatible with what we would expect on the basis of the stories we hear, both in terms of problems and successes. Susan Karlson, while serving as an intern minister with our four hundred-member Unitarian Universalist Church of Annapolis, Maryland, gathered information about its covenant group program during its first year, which began in January 2001. This program was unusual in that it used a trimester system, asking four-month commitments from those joining covenant groups. It also began with cofacilitators for each group. There were six covenant groups in the church after a bit more than a year.

Karlson found plenty of good news in what the Annapolis folks had to say. Covenant groups, for example, were "becoming increasingly important aspects of the group members' lives." A basic goal of covenant groups was being met, it seems, because survey respondents praised the "sharing, mutual respect and developing friendships" of their groups. They approved of what they called "increased spirituality," adding that they liked the "relaxed and comfortable environments" of their covenant groups. Even the overall structure of Small Group Ministry, Karlson found, "was rated very positively," including "regular meetings and schedules, expected attendance, support and understanding, and limited membership (maximum of ten people in each group)." Obviously, the covenant group program at this church had been successfully launched.

Still, there were some problem areas. Two of them may be instructive for Small Group Ministry leaders in other congregations: the need for greater clarity about the purpose of covenant groups and a shortfall in the acceptance of covenants for service beyond the group itself.

Clarity of Purpose

Some of the "confusion about the nature of covenant groups" that Karlson found in the Annapolis church's program was deep-seated: "Some people thought more structure was needed while others wanted to see their groups alternate between structure and free-flowing discussion. Some emphasized the discussion nature of their group while others stated that they knew that the group was not intended to just be a discussion group." Karlson concludes, "Covenant groups need to be explained better, so that people know what to expect."

Other congregations have found similar problems. Sometimes covenant group leaders take too little time to explain the purpose of covenant groups, and sometimes members fail to understand it. Jonalu Johnstone, of First Unitarian Church of Oklahoma City, has been serving part-time in the smaller, nearby Channing

Unitarian Universalist Church of Edmond, which had "covenant groups" in place when she arrived. She says,

> When people here first heard about covenant groups, they tried to make everything be a covenant group. It took a couple years to let that unwind and for them to realize that every group (the Women's Lunch, Dining Out, the Choir) didn't *have* to be a covenant group, and that it would be good to be deliberate in identifying covenant groups as covenant groups and letting the others go on being what they are.

Don Skinner, lay leader of the Connection Circles program at the Shawnee Mission Unitarian Universalist Church in Oakland Park, Kansas, stresses how important it is to take care in spelling out to people considering covenant group membership exactly what is expected and what they are getting into. That will not always be enough, though, because problems don't always come from a failure to clearly communicate the purpose of Small Group Ministry. Even when the purpose has been made clear, Skinner finds, "some will not buy into the full program. Especially some older folks. We have had to ask some people to withdraw when it became apparent they did not plan to come regularly and were treating the group in a casual manner." A Small Group Ministry leader in a Southwest congregation told me, "Some of our leaders are over-complicating this or letting the groups redefine the purpose as something other than relational. Some of our facilitators are listening to a few group members who don't want a relational group."

Molly Scott, a Small Group Ministry leader at the Community Church of New York City, reports that one of that congregation's covenant groups did not follow the recommended format and "just discussed politics." Participants in that group "did not bond the way the others have," she added, and the group did not last. Duane Fickeisen, cominister of the Unitarian Universalists of Cumberland Valley in Boiling Springs, Pennsylvania, says that two groups there failed to gel because "a few participants took their commitments casually, showing up when they felt like it or when they didn't have something better to do, thus frustrating the other members."

Covenants to Serve Church and Community

The second all-too-common problem Karlson found in her covenant group study became apparent in responses to a question about the covenant group's larger-community service project. "What project?" was one answer. Another respondent said, "We don't have a project and never discussed it." One person, who credited covenant group participation with her greater sense of connectedness to the church, complained that "the service project feels more like a formal obligation." Karlson concluded, "There is a source of tension in the idea of service projects that needs to be explored, to make the service more meaningful or enriching for the church and the covenant group members."

The Unitarian Universalists of Cumberland Valley also resisted doing service projects during the first year, Fickeisen said, although service was "an explicit expectation." As the second year began, a couple of the groups did service projects for the church. In congregations where covenants to serve others are being made and kept, service to the church seems to be far more frequent than service to the larger community. Here, from other congregations, are some examples of responses to the expectation of covenants of service:

- All of the service projects of Channing Unitarian Universalist Church, when Johnstone wrote about them not long ago, had been for the church itself: "The Artists Group is putting together the Fall Fair (a fundraiser). The Stitchers (used to be Quilters) has made Christmas stockings for all the children of the church and made the church banner. The Book Group has done a worship service. The Gaia Group plans to do a worship service."
- "Some groups have done significant service projects," Skinner reports from Shawnee Mission, "such as running the annual service auction. Another has taken on fixing up our playground. Overall, the leaders have been great."
- Dr. Greta Fryxell, facilitator of the Music Covenant Group in the Wildflower Church, Austin, Texas, was pleasantly surprised at how well the group fit into the formation of this still-gathering congregation. Singing "speaks to our hearts," she says, as well as "our desire to serve the church." She adds, "I am strengthened when I see the spirits of people lift as they come into one of our services and hear the singers from the Music Covenant Group belting out a welcome. It does put across a message."

But what of service to the larger community? If there is any substantial number of wonderful projects being aided by Small Group Ministries today, we Unitarian Universalists are being uncharacteristically modest, hiding our good works under bushel baskets.

Covenants

There are groups claiming to be covenant groups that not only ignore the expectation of covenants to serve others but also the need for a covenant of behavior within their own groups. Connie Strait, of Unity Temple Unitarian Universalist Congregation of Oak Park, Illinois, a 350-member congregation with 80 persons in covenant groups, reported that only some of the church's nine groups had taken the time to agree to covenants of group behavior: "Some have. Others are a bit resistant." When Skinner was asked whether the Shawnee Mission small groups have created covenants of behavior, he answered, "Sort of. We could have been more deliberate about it." Gabriel Gelb, of Emerson Unitarian Church in Houston, which has six covenant groups, had a short answer to the same question: "No." Joel Ross, of the Unitarian Universalist Church of Livermore, California, had an equally short answer about that church's two groups: "Yes." A more complex, and perhaps more typical, answer came from Nathan Stone of the Unitarian Universalist Fellowship of Waco, Texas. About behavioral covenants in that church's six covenant groups, Stone wrote, "This is definitely the hard part—actually hammering out and fine tuning the covenant. It takes lots of energy, but this covenant process is what covenant groups are about. In the process deep friendships are made." Stone enjoys his role as leader of the Facilitators' Covenant Group because he and others always leave feeling uplifted: "We think it is because the Facilitators' Group 'gets it,' the concept, the importance of the covenant, and that friendship, not any topic, is why we are there."

At the CCV Practitioners Summit, Cheryl Ring, of the Unitarian Universalist congregation in Augusta, Maine, offered still more positive examples from her church. She talked about the fact that when the church was beginning its Small Group Ministries, discussion of covenants made clear that what the church was starting were "relational groups," meaning that people would be expected to make some commitments, including listening to each other. "We talk about the need for facilitators and that in every group there needs to be a covenant," she said. "The covenant is as close as we get to having rules." It is also perhaps as close as we get to an absolute requirement for a group's calling itself a *covenant group*.

Reaching Out to Those Who Need Us

As we saw in an earlier chapter, one of the most serious not-yet-solved problems of Small Group Ministry is making our covenant groups open to new folks. It is a problem likely to be with us for a while, and it is not ours alone. "What is the biggest issue on which people disagree regarding small groups?" asked Michael Mack, an advisor to evangelical Christian churches. In a 1996 essay posted on the Internet, Mack answered his own question: "Whether groups should be open or closed."

The issue isn't one of knowing what to do. Churches of other denominations already are using Small Group Ministry's power to welcome and integrate new people into their churches. Their methods are not secret, and they are not theology dependent. Jan Koons, who has been successful in leading small group growth at Desert Cross Lutheran Church in Tempe, Arizona, recently laid out the elements of his success in five easy tips in an article on the Stephens Ministry web page:

- Put birthing into the covenant as the goal of the group.
- Encourage members to invite people visitors.
- Have apprentices training to be facilitators.
- When the group nears maximum size, let the facilitator move on to a different time or location to start a new group, leaving the apprentice in charge of the original group.
- Ask existing group members to realize that they will not hurt anyone's feelings if they switch to the new group.

These measures, Koons says, are "painful in the short term, but positive in the long run." He adds, "The key to birthing is attitude. Birthing is a chance to grow, individually, as a group, and as a congregation. It succeeds when people view it as something positive."

But our covenant group members, thus far, generally do not view birthing of new groups as something positive. In Annapolis, Karlson found, splitting groups "seems frightening to most people." Skinner puts it bluntly: "Covenant groups refuse to split. We have to form new groups." That appears to be the nearest thing we have to a solution to date: Allow covenant groups with the maximum number of members to become closed until natural attrition provides openings, and at the same time start new groups for people who want places in our covenant group meetings. So far, we haven't found a better way.

Minor Variations on the Norm

Some of the standard Small Group Ministry recommendations are obviously less crucial than the expectation that covenant groups will have covenants and less worrisome than our reluctance to spin off new covenant groups to make space for more participants. Apprentice facilitators are said to be a significant component of covenant groups, for example, but it is not clear how many covenant groups have a full complement of apprentices in place. It may be that more groups, like those in Annapolis, have cofacilitators, and it is a fact that some have neither cofacilitators nor apprentices.

It is also recommended that covenant groups beyond the pilot program stage commit to meeting for at least a church year. The Annapolis congregation, as it began its second year in this program, was having some success with four-month commitments, and Community Church of New York City starts new groups about twice a year, asking members for three months of commitment each time, after which covenant groups decide whether or not to continue.

Although covenant group meetings may take place in churches, we have encouraged in-home meetings, which do seem to be the norm in our congregations. About half of the Small Group Ministries in Calvin Dame's church, though, meet in the church building. And in some circumstances, the church is the only reasonable choice. Molly Scott says meetings in her New York City church's building are what make that congregation's four covenant groups viable, because members live too far apart in too many sections of the city for regular in-home meetings to be practical. To get from her home to the home of one other member of her covenant group, Scott says, she would have to take two buses, the subway, and a boat, which would take a total of about two hours each way. The church building is more centrally located. Research, in this case, produced a wise deviation from our norm. Scott said,

> Prior to our starting our first groups I had talked with the person at Marble Collegiate Church (Reformed Church in America) here in Manhattan where they have had similar groups for ten to twelve years and they have all their groups at the church and so we decided to go that route. Some groups have chosen to have special events at members' homes, but they all meet most of the time at the church.

Church Size and Covenant Groups

Different sizes of churches require different organizational structures and make different sorts of demands on ministers, so we shouldn't be surprised if the problems and successes of Small Group Ministries differ across church sizes in our Association.

Church size may need to be taken into account as we consider the future of covenant groups in our Association.

Turner has speculated that Small Group Ministry may be most difficult for small fellowships (150 members or fewer) that lack professional ministry, and these groups might have special problems. It could be that the characteristics of both midsize (150–550 members) and small churches make Small Group Ministry more a means of enhancing the experience of the current membership than a way of reaching out to others in our larger communities. If so, that's not a bad result. It is, however, much less than the best that one could imagine.

Robinson fears that the comforts of the not-large will lead some of our midsize congregations to settle for creating a few covenant groups and avoiding effective outreach. At the Practitioners' Summit he said,

> A pastoral church may have three or four or five. We can have a portion of the church in covenant groups but we won't transform the church. This will strengthen the church, it will bring a sense of community to those folks who are participating in covenant groups, and it may even change the culture. But the church will stay a pastoral church. The lay people and the minister will still collaborate to keep it a pastoral church.

Or the covenant group movement could lead such a church to make the jump to a significantly higher level by planning for and creating twenty or thirty new covenant groups, as the Brewster church did at one crucial juncture.

Perhaps it was the difficulty of being the minister of an in-between, midsize church that caused Dame to say recently,

> My experience is that our churches are hell bent on staying comfortable, which is to say, staying the same size that they have always been. And you have to give credit where credit is due: they are really good at it. An important part of the problem that we have to address is the fact—and I am sorry to say this—our churches do not want to grow.

Some people believe that midsize churches such as Dame's are an endangered species in today's world. Johnstone, while she was growth consultant for the Southwest District, studied the membership totals of our 70 or so congregations in the district and found that congregations with between 150 and 550 adults lost ground during the 1990s. What little growth the district experienced came from new starts and large congregations. Midsize churches may have especially difficult aspects.

Stefan Jonasson, the UUA coordinator of services to large churches, sees great benefits for the midsize church in Small Group Ministry. Midsize churches often put time and money into adult education programs, which offer some of the possibilities for friendship building that covenant groups do. For less effort and less expenditure, Jonasson says, Small Group Ministries can serve the same purposes better.

Michael McGee, who leads a ministry team for a congregation of more than a thousand adult members, thinks the covenant group movement is going to live or die in our large churches, and he thinks those churches are moving in the direction of using Small Group Ministry as a means of genuine reform. "I think the ministers of our large churches realize this is what they have to do to make the large church work," he says. And he is optimistic enough to add, "I think as the large churches succeed with covenant groups, the other churches are going to see that success and follow suit. When others see this working for large churches, they'll give it a try."

Jonasson, who works closely with our ministers of large churches, agrees that our congregations of 550 or more will have the easiest path to full and effective Small Group Ministry. Ministers of large churches are accustomed to being more like administrators than pastors, he notes, and covenant groups offer large churches a solution to one of their major problems: that members of large churches can be lost in the crowd without connection to others. "Big and impersonal" is the rap against many of our larger congregations, and Small Group Ministry offers a way to make that charge less valid.

Benefits for Our Children

We have much to learn about how to use Small Group Ministry for the benefit of our children. Applications of Small Group Ministry to children and youth are being tried now in various congregations. Gail Forsyth-Vail, a religious educator at our North Parish Church in North Andover, Massachusetts, and Helen Zidowecki, a religious education consultant for the UUA's Northeast District, have been working, together and separately, on covenant group use in their programs for many months.

Whereas most other church school programs have teachers and curricula, the North Parish Church sessions have adult group leaders whose primary role is "encouraging and facilitating connections" and a combination of worship and small groups. Forsyth-Vail's religious education program applies covenant group techniques to groups ranging in size, ideally, from eight to twelve children. Each group has a maximum size of ten in the lower grades, but space problems currently dictate groups of up to fifteen for older children. Following "Safe Church" policy, Forsyth-Vail requires that two adult facilitators be present in each group at all times.

After a worship service for children in grades one through eight, the covenant group meetings begin with an opening game or a check-in. Then there is a period of reflection, with questions or activities related to the worship service. A ten- to twenty-minute period called "Carrying Our Faith into the World" follows. This time can involve a service project or a consideration of how values can be put into practice. The last few minutes are devoted to closing expressions of appreciation or wishes for how things might have been different. Then the children help clean up the space and restore it to how it was when they arrived.

Moving to this approach required some difficult decisions on the part of North Andover's religious education leaders, and a big decision was forgoing curricula. Two recognitions led to the change. One, Forsyth-Vail says, was the recognition that the church was losing the participation of lots of children and that it was, for children—as is the case for adults—relationships that held the ones who stayed. The other recognition was that Forsyth-Vail felt much more comfortable than some lay teachers about dealing with Judeo-Christian religious beliefs. Group worship now takes the place of what had been the core religious education material. Through an adaptation of covenant groups, Forsyth-Vail says, the North Andover program has shifted its focus to "what no one else can do for our children, spiritual development." North Andover's minister, Lee Bluemel, sees two additional benefits to Forsythe-Vail's approach to religious education. The "Coming of Age" program for teenagers is working "wonderfully well," she says, as a covenant group with Bluemel as facilitator. And when the church moved to two Sunday morning services, the modular covenant group religious education program was flexible enough to adjust to the change with relative ease. With three covenant groups for third-through fifth-graders, for example, Forsyth-Vail put one in the early service time slot and two in the later service period.

In her role in the NE District, Zidowecki promotes Small Group Ministry for all ages. "Small Group Ministry has the potential to transform the educational ministry of the church," she writes in *Covenant Group News,* noting that children identify with a church in stages. They begin by identifying with people in the church; then they identify with the place, claiming it as "their church"; and finally they get to "name recognition and the meanings and learnings that accompany that recognition." Adults, she adds, go through the same stages.

A Way to Keep Our Young Folk With Us

By 2010, we may know how to keep our young folk from disappearing from our churches after high school. Peter Bowden and members of the First Unitarian Church of Providence, Rhode Island, launched a Small Group Ministry in February 2002. A religious education workshop led by Zidowecki and Dame inspired Bowden to work toward an integration of young adult groups and this program. He calls covenant groups *youth groups for adults* because of similarities between the Small Group Ministry format and many youth group programs that have been operating for years. The pilot Young Adult Covenant Group Bowden facilitated in Providence continued to meet twice a month through the program's first summer. "Do you understand how powerful this is?" he asked in an e-mail. "Even though church had gone into summer mode, our Small Group Ministry kept going. The consensus is that it will go on forever."

The Young Adult Covenant Groups in Providence are grouped by age. Bowden says this system allows for entire groups to gradually "age out" of the young adult program and move on together, into the church's ongoing adult Small Group Ministries. This arrangement, he says, represents a major change. Up until now, members of our youth programs have graduated out and found nothing offered to them except Sunday morning worship services. He finds it not at all surprising that we have lost so many at that transition point. Bowden writes,

> How can we expect them to be happy with worship alone after such a powerful experience? I went to college and didn't think twice about going to church. I had no interest. I had never been before, except for holidays. Why start? I did have interest in a youth-group-like experience, but I assumed that wasn't offered for people my age. I was jealous of the fellowship and depth of community in the many Bible groups scattered throughout our dorm complex. If there had been a Unitarian Universalist equivalent where we could have gathered and reflected, explored, and shared in a structured way, I would have jumped at it. Didn't happen. Years later I ended up back in Providence and became a youth advisor, an adult supporting the best form of ministry I know.

Having experienced the power of youth programs and the continuity Small Group Ministry offers young adults, Bowden believes all congregations should adopt what he calls "the winning combination of small groups and celebratory worship." And, he says, "We need to publicize it, make sure our youth and young adults know both aspects of good church are there for them, and prepare to see our faith grow like mad. I hope that my yet-to-be children will be able to go anywhere in the Unitarian Universalist universe and find a Covenant Group Ministry program waiting for them."

A Way to Reach Across Geographic Boundaries

Within this decade, we should know whether Small Group Ministry can work without meetings. Although that idea may seem as strange as the idea of a covenant-free covenant group, meeting-free Small Group Ministry may (or may not) be possible because of e-mail. Our Boston-based Church of the Larger Fellowship (CLF) is studying the success of an e-mail covenant group begun about two years ago by Rebecca Vinson, of North Carolina, and Tom Little, of New Mexico. As a congregation serving isolated Unitarian Universalists through mail, telephone, and e-mail, CLF is considering whether e-mail covenant groups are a logical and effective step in the church's evolution.

Vinson, after having led a covenant group for the Eno River Fellowship in Durham, North Carolina, and being "thrilled with the results," had participated in CLF and UUA-sponsored e-mail lists and electronic bulletin boards because her husband's military career had taken them to places far from any Unitarian Universalist church. Unable to get a CLF e-mail list to work as she wished it to, she wrote something that brought an offer of help from Little, a member of the Unitarian Church of Los Alamos, New Mexico. Little set up a covenant group via Yahoo Group's free service, and he and Vinson co-lead it. Describing herself as the apprentice on the team with Little, Vinson also leads another e-mail covenant group by herself.

Here is how these CLF-encouraged e-mail covenant groups work: A topic is announced via e-mail, and the resulting discussion proceeds on a three-week cycle. When a group member sends an e-mail message to the appropriate Yahoo address, it is automatically forwarded to all other members and archived. Vinson describes one on-line, three-week, covenant group session: "The first day of the first week Opening Words are sent to everyone and then check-in begins. It takes at least a week for everyone to check in. Often discussions begin about topics raised in people's check-ins. Topic discussion takes about two weeks. Then closing words are posted and the cycle begins again the following week."

Keeping a group on track may be more difficult on-line than in person. Vinson notes that topics growing out of check-in sometimes become the focus of discussion in place of the topic that some members have been looking forward to discussing. So far, the groups have not closed with expressions of likes and wishes, as some face-to-face covenant groups do, but Vinson expects to add that soon.

Keeping group size to ten or fewer members is as important on-line as in person, Vinson believes, but the problem of what to do when that size is reached may be no easier in cyberspace. When one of her groups reached ten members a couple of years ago, some members felt the group was too new to spawn off another group, and others expressed anxiety about losing contact with those in the group they'd only recently come to know. Decisions about how to deal with these familiar complaints were avoided when two members dropped out. "Did those two leave because the group refused to split? Or did their departure prove it was wise not to split because new members had just joined and might not stay with us?" So far, Vinson can only say, "Don't know yet."

The benefits covenant group members get from "meeting" by e-mail seem to be similar to the benefits enjoyed by traditional covenant groups. A member of Vinson's first covenant group, Kim Barra, who found Unitarian Universalism by visiting the UUA web site, says,

> What I love most about this group is the opportunity to get to know Unitarian Universalists from different parts of the country, different backgrounds, and different spiritual orientations. The nature of our small group and the regularity of our communications have enabled us to develop a sense of familiarity, even intimacy, as we discuss various topics from our individual Unitarian Universalist perspectives.

E-mail covenant groups are already serving well the needs of some people. They offer the possibility of reaching folks we might never know otherwise and gaining the enrichment of their presence, if only electronically. One critic, though, has expressed the concern that on-line covenant groups might allow some people to avoid face-to-face contact, to their own detriment. Also, CLF leaders recognize that there are some other issues to be worked out. How are facilitators of such groups to be chosen and trained? Will the facilitators "meet" regularly in a covenant group of their own with the minister of CLF? How are the group-service components of

Covenant Group Ministry to be fulfilled? How deep can the sharing of life stories safely be when that sharing occurs in e-mail messages that can be forwarded at will and stored, essentially, forever? At this point we can only echo what Vinson said about how on-line covenant groups will deal with growth and the ten-member limit: "Don't know yet."

Where will we have been by 2010? Don't know that yet, either, of course. The trip, though, looks interesting from here.

Principle, Compassion, Openness and Hope

The hugely successful Fellowship Church in Grapevine, Texas, has something we Unitarian Universalists are glad we don't have: dogma. Fellowship Church's "Statement of Faith" ends by saying that "the Bible is God's word to all men. . . . Because it is inspired by God, it is truth without any mixture of error." While the minister of Fellowship Church may be casually dressed as he roams around the church's stage before as many as three thousand in a Saturday or Sunday service, his church claims to offer absolute truth of the sort expressed by a bumper sticker I once saw on a Texas car: "God said it, I believe it, and that's that."

We Unitarian Universalists have lacked that kind of certainty at least since 1819, when William Ellery Channing declared it our duty to bring to our reading of the Bible one of God's gifts to humankind: our minds. Biblical inerrancy has never been a core belief of ours, and no Unitarian Universalist wants dogma at the center of our faith. Still, many of us are struggling with a perceived need for a more deeply held and widely shared vision for Unitarian Universalism, and we are puzzled by our failure to reach more than a tiny fraction of those in our communities who need liberal religion. Well over thirty-two million people live in the four states of the Southwest District. How can it be that fewer than ten thousand of them are Unitarian Universalist?

A group of Houston-area ministers who had gathered for a Unitarian Universalist Ministers Association chapter meeting in May 2000 took seriously a question raised by planners of a convocation. What, they were asked, are the "pressing issues" of Unitarian Universalism today? The ministers replied, "We have no credible eschatology, no motivating vision of a future that calls to us, pulling us forward. Faced with immense global problems, we have no Unitarian Universalist response based on a compelling sense of purpose."

The explanatory sentence that accompanied that bleak statement follows:

> Working, as we do, in the midst of the tension between individual freedom and community values, and aware of the implications of environmental destruction connected with the increasing pressures of population growth and economic expansion, we are not sure how to do effective social justice ministry in and/or through our churches, although some of us see hope in the possibilities of small-group organization.

How do we, an association of churches populated by folks who are theologically diverse, articulate, and highly opinionated, get to a vision of a future capable of calling us forward? Faced with global problems so immense that we may be wrecking the environment that sustains us, the habitat of our grandchildren and future generations, how do we discover and agree upon a plan of action that can offer hope and a sense of purpose? How may we accomplish all this without tearing our diverse congregations to shreds?

Covenant Group Faith

We know we need such a unifying vision. We also know we cannot and should not ignore the fundamental theological and philosophical differences that exist within our membership, but few of us believe we can debate our way to agreement. No amount of arguing under *Robert's Rules of Order* will take us to consensus on a compelling purpose for our faith. Severe repression might. A new McCarthy Era enhanced by modern surveillance techniques could perhaps focus us on a defense of basic freedoms while we set aside our disagreements. Covenant groups could serve us well in the various worst-case scenarios we can imagine. But even in this threatened, but blessedly still free, nation, Small Group Ministry opens to us a better way of relating than we have known before. By listening to each other's concerns and joys in covenant groups and helping each other with our struggles to make it through one more day, we are now able to build within our churches the sort of mutual trust that puts into compassionate perspective the profound differences in our understandings of our lives, of life.

Lacking thus far a "Unitarian Universalist response based on a compelling sense of purpose," we seem to be near agreement on a stage-on-the-way, a procedural vision. Soon Small Group Ministry will be so widespread among us that we may generally agree on the following:

> When a small group of Unitarian Universalists meets together regularly with a facilitator and a format that encourages listening and the sharing of feelings and ideas, they will deepen their commitment to each other, to their church, and to Unitarian Universalism; they will be more likely to become effective workers for change in their larger communities; and they will get more from being part of their church than they ever have before.

Does this turning of our attention to a form of church organization mean that we are abandoning deeper issues, averting our eyes from the most profound questions of being mortal human beings? No. This way of being with one another requires respectful attention to others and implies recognition of what some Buddhists refer to as "basic goodness" in our fellow human beings. Community, being together in right relationship, is the wellspring of religion. Beneath our differences, we can recognize what we have in common: deep needs, strength, courage, and wisdom. Small Group Ministry, Thandeka believes, provides "sacred space" in which we may practice right relationship as a sacramental act. During a recent General Assembly workshop, she said:

> As Unitarian Universalists, we know this sacred space when two or more persons gather together as a ritual practice of right relationship. We know it as the healing and transformational power of life itself. We are transformed by this act into a religious people, a people whose purposes and principles explain and affirm this sacramental act of right relationship. When we accept one another openheartedly, we feel the presence of life in a human embrace.

Small Group Ministry works, she says, because each covenant group session is a liturgy that creates an open space for opened hearts.

Right Relationship

Our making a practice of right relationship begins with attentive listening and recognizes that all human understanding, even our own, is incomplete in fundamental ways. Much of what we know through our senses has the value of being verifiable, but it is also limited. Dogs hear and smell what we don't, and bees see aspects of reality that we cannot. The ways we humans differ from one another are less hard-wired, but we know, intellectually at least, how deeply all our understandings have been shaped by particular genetic, environmental, and cultural influences of our lives. Our perceptions, as William S. Hill argued in his philosophy of science work, are theory-laden. In other words, what we can notice and make sense of depends in large measure on what we already understand to be true. No wonder we differ. Many Unitarian Universalists are people who, having reasoned and argued our way out of other religions, are proud of the belief structures we've carved out for ourselves, of how far we've come.

Covenant groups are a transformational practice through which we, with others, can discover our own underlying assumptions about reality and examine our ways of being, some of which have become so habitual that they seem to us just "the way things are." The practice of Small Group Ministry does not ask us to deny our own understandings of reality, but it does ask us to suspend judgment long enough to hear respectfully the understandings of others, even those vastly different from our own. First, hear and understand. This basic requirement of Small Group Ministry is a fundamental step in the practice of right relationship, and it is, as Thandeka recognizes, a sacramental act. It also may be a necessary first step in our being able to move with power in the direction of humankind's evolutionary journey away from the abyss of environmental disaster.

When we know another deeply, we are less likely to be offended by his or her failure to see the wisdom of our own beliefs about God or spirituality or abortion or applications of genetic technology or globalism or responses to terrorism. When we are known deeply, we can say what we believe with less fear of giving offense. Disagreements of congregation-rending intensity can be handled within the confines of covenant groups without either equivocation or the kind of hurt that can cause people to go away and not come back. How many profound issues will we Unitarian Universalists be called upon to struggle with this year, next year, and in the coming decade? Every day presents us with scores of issues capable of dividing our churches into feuding factions if we seek to debate our way to common agreement.

The changes Small Group Ministry brings to Unitarian Universalism are as tactical as they are generous. Backus, the lay member of our congregation in Tacoma, Washington, describes his church's mission as being well beyond inward-focused self-care. Its mission, Backus said, is "to connect people in small groups for worship, compassion, study, and service, to foment a change in the way we view the planet and the way we live. To change a congregation of members into a world of ministers." Would not such a change be revolutionary in most of our churches? Backus thinks Small Group Ministry is "the only way to have a revolution," promising, as it does, to bring to us fundamental change without the confrontational, public-arena debates of earlier times.

Barbara J. Pescan of the Unitarian Church of Evanston, Illinois, in her "Service of the Living Tradition" sermon at the 2002 General Assembly, said,

> It is more than time to put aside semantic wrangling over differences so we can pay attention to the similarities among us. . . . Lest our unitary and universal ideas become quaint anachronisms, it is time to relinquish our closely held and vaunted differences and look across religions and cultures for what unites us.

Citing a version of "Let My Little Light Shine" that ends "May be someone down in the valley, tryin' to get home," Pescan concluded,

> It is time to aim our lights down there into the valley where someone, surely, is trying to get home, trying to get over, trying to get out of trouble, trying to get on to the morning. It is time to lift our lights and our eyes. It may be we have been focusing our vision too low. It may be . . . that we have spent too much of our time preaching against the critic in the front row and too little listening to the hunger of those in the back, who are ready to go on and go out with the message if only someone would remind them often enough why they should.

Why should those in the back who know spiritual hunger go out with the message of our free faith? Because there are literally millions around us who need liberal religion. In his *UU World* column after the General Assembly, our president, Bill Sinkford, cited Pescan's sermon as a highlight of the assembly for him, and he, too, directed our attention to those down in the valley trying to get home. Sinkford said that when he is asked why growth in Unitarian Universalism is important, he finds the answer to be simple:

> Our commitment to growth must flow from that place where our love for this faith encounters the aching needs of the world. Thousands of people—tens of thousands—yearn for what we have found. Many who don't know about us have given up hope of finding a community of faith that values real, lived human experience.

These are people with concerns and attitudes remarkably like our own. Ray says they are all around us, all around our churches. "We're not the Lone Rangers any more," Davidson Loehr, minister of First Unitarian Church of Austin, Texas, said in a sermon on Cultural Creatives. "There are about fifty million of us." And then he asked a question that needs to be heard throughout Unitarian Universalism and beyond: "What if our mission is . . . to save the world and our most sacred task is to get about the business of discovering, together, how to do it?"

To call attention to our faith's shortcomings or to note that we lack a sufficient, unifying, vision capable of drawing us forward is not to say that Unitarian Universalism is without virtue and strength. Far from it. We are a religion of tolerance guided by principle, compassion, openness to change, and hope.

Mary Harrington, minister of the Unitarian Universalist Church of Marblehead, Massachusetts, included in a recent sermon a story about a time when she experienced the unique value of the nondogmatic faith we call our own. Harrington was working many years ago as a parish minister and as a chaplain at a Catholic hospital when a nurse there killed her husband and herself. Harrington was asked by hospital authorities to meet the next morning with the woman's co-workers and to offer them support and grief counseling. She relates,

> Knowing the staff came from many different denominations, they decided to ask me because they said they trusted that I would be able to hear and be there for everybody. They chose me, over their own priests and nuns, over the other Protestant chaplains who worked there, because I, as a Unitarian Universalist minister, could be counted on to just show up and love everyone. To not offer explanations or platitudes that might comfort some but would alienate others. To go with an open heart and be present to people in their anguish and guilt and total bafflement.

After the bereaved family's minister refused to officiate at a memorial service for a murderer and suicide victim, Harrington was asked to do that, too. "Because of our faith, I could [do that service]. And even though it was so hard and part of me really didn't want to, because of our faith, I did." In the service she said:

God wants us to love life and each other and to love ourselves. The world needs each of us, depends on each of us, to live in harmony, not only with each other in our workplace and community, but also within our own hearts and souls. It is essential for the wholeness of all beings—because we are inextricably connected to each other—for each of us to reach out, and reach in.

As heartening as this story of religion based in "real, lived human experience" is, we should note that even as we move away from the worst of our divisive contentiousness, if Harrington had expressed such sentiments in the context of some of our churches or fellowships, she might well have been challenged by at least a few parishioners asking, "Oh, you don't still believe that, do you?" The risk of incurring such responses has kept many of us quiet about our deepest beliefs, throwing us into a "don't ask, don't tell" approach to our experiences of, and thoughts about, what is most profound. We are coming to recognize that Universalists during the premerger decades were not notably successful in arguing people into the comforting arms of a universally forgiving God and that we've had no greater success with forums pitting our most vocal Unitarian Universalist thinkers against each other in debates that may be well reasoned but are also usually egocentric and repetitious. Who wants to join a fight in progress? No one we'd want as a member.

If we allow Small Group Ministry to change the culture of Unitarian Universalism, we may find the truth of what liberal religious folk for so long have claimed to believe: Revelation is not sealed. Reality-changing insights remain possible. Within the minimal structure of the covenant group, we can reflect upon our own motivations, confront and refine our emotions, consider our ethics, deepen our attentiveness to others, cultivate wisdom, and express our love through service. Most of us are Cultural Creatives. Speaking as one himself, Ray has said,

We are part of the movements who cared heavily about science and consciousness and personal transformation and alternative healing . . . the environmental movement, the women's movement, jobs in social justice, the peace movement, the civil rights movement, the organic food and alternative health-care movements, and all the different spiritual movements.

All of these movements, he says, are "converging right now toward a single new phenomenon we're calling a wisdom culture." Unitarian Universalists sharing those concerns and focused through attentive listening to what matters most to the human soul can be leaders of a wisdom culture, the emergence of which is desperately needed. We are remarkably creative people capable of producing inspiring results when we are in circumstances that allow us to function at our best.

To be at our best, though, most of us need to feel welcomed. "Hospitality," Johnstone has said with evident irony, "is such a wonderful concept." Johnstone has devoted much of her professional life to encouraging our congregations to make hospitality more than a concept. She knows that when hospitality has truly become our practice, we may become able to spread it to our neighborhoods and beyond. In words permanently enshrined in the back of our hymnal, former UUA president Bill Schulz says, "This is the mission of our faith: to teach the fragile art of hospitality."

Fortunately, the fragile art of hospitality can be learned. Having practiced among ourselves hospitality's most essential element, attending to others, and having received from others the blessings of respectful attention, we can become more generously hospitable to those needing a way out of the valleys into which all lives sometimes slip.

When Small Group Ministry has become predominant in our churches, when there are enough covenant groups all over this continent and in our societies elsewhere in the world, we will evolve a vision capable of drawing us forward together toward peace and a sustainable life for humankind on earth. Having failed to talk our way there, we may listen our way to a vision that will allow us to lend our weight to the forces seeking a culture of enlightened wisdom. Covenant groups are compassion in practice, tolerance guided by principle; the mutual trust they foster will lead us to change. Through compassionate hospitality, we may, ten people at a time, help to save the world.

Sample Materials

Sample Brochure for Small Group Ministry

What Is Small Group Ministry?

Small Group Ministry is a network of small groups, whose main objectives are to strengthen the congregation by drawing us into mutual ministry.

Why are we developing Small Group Ministry in our congregation?

We expect through Small Group Ministry to continuously develop lay leadership, deepen our understanding of Unitarian-Universalist principles and values, be further challenged to action and spiritual growth, as well as to be prompted to express, in a more consistent way, our principles and values in the community.

Tell me more about these ministry groups!

The primary emphasis of Small Group Ministry is to care for people—to serve them, encourage them to spiritual growth, and meet their needs for affirmation and acceptance. By creating an open, supportive, and nurturing environment, Small Group Ministry promotes and facilitates spiritual growth and mutual interactive care for one another, therefore providing a quality of caring that most people can only wish for.

Additionally, Small Group Ministry offers opportunities to search and grow at the individual's own pace and in the individual's own way through learning together and loving one another. As individuals identify and use their own spiritual gifts, they will be moved to contribute of themselves and their resources.

When are we going to begin the Small Group Ministry in our congregation?

Signups will begin on Sunday, September 30. The small groups will begin meeting starting Sunday, October 21.

How can I be involved?

There are several ways in which you can be involved in Small Group Ministry: As an Small Group Ministry Council member, as a Leader or Coleader of a small group, and as a group member. Any way you are able to, or at any time you decide to participate, your involvement will be always welcome.

—First Unitarian Church, San Jose, California

Sample Brochure for Small Group Ministry

Purpose

To provide an opportunity for friends and members of the church to develop deeper connections and wider service within the church community through small-group organization.

Goals

1. To provide regular opportunities for lifting one's mental/emotional horizons up from the mundane considerations of day-to-day life.

2. And, in the relative safety of carefully-led small groups, to help people get to know and be known by up to 10 others with similar interests.

About the Groups

- These small groups meet a minimum of once a month in a member's home or at the church.

- All groups have trained facilitators, use a regular format, and covenant together how they will relate to each other and how they will serve the congregation.

- Groups are always open to new members.

Groups are developed around topics of interest to members and friends of the church.

Conscious Consuming: Learn what it takes to make the goods we crave, and how to make more socially responsible spending choices. Facilitator: Kari Darken-Thompson

Cooking: We believe that food provides social and spiritual as well as physical nourishment when it is shared. Share current life experiences and food, followed by a discussion of the recipe and related topics. Facilitators: Mike Brown and Alan Hart

Deep Listening: Explore individual life journeys through shared thoughts and experiences. Facilitator: Corie Haring

Dialogues: The group aims beyond debate and discussion, and strives for genuine dialogue. The participants work as hard at listening as at speaking. The topics flow freely, but in its best moments, the group achieves a genuine intimacy through dialogue. Facilitator: Jim Gordon

Experience Art: A safe, nurturing place to make art. Facilitator: Maureen Harvey

Explore and Celebrate Diversity: Discussion of topics related to gay, lesbian, bisexual, and transgender issues in a safe, nurturing environment. Facilitator: Laura Hanson

Exploring Creativity: This group will explore the creative process. How does creativity enhance your daily life, your interests, and learning? Facilitator: Gene Roseboom

Exploring Spirituality: We explore various spiritual practices and ideas in a safe, nurturing environment. Facilitator: Margaret Roseboom

Fabric Artistry: Discuss, share, and work on projects. Participants bring their own sewing, quilting, and fabric art projects. Facilitator: Ann McDermott

Movie Discussion: Like movies? Like to talk about them? Join this group. Facilitators: Debbie Allen and Deidra Murray

Music Group: Music is a sacred experience to many UUs in this church. This group provides a place to perform and share all kinds of music with each other. Facilitator: Bob Hurst

Parenting: Facilitator: Pam Yarbrough

Sacred Treasures: We explore our spiritual lives. We include a time of silence during each meeting, often share poetry and music that is meaningful to us, and address the topics that group members find compelling. Facilitator: Wil Scott

Sound, Movement, Touch, and Breath: Facilitator: Marne Harveland-Botkin

Spiritual Journeys: We share our individual spiritual journeys. How did you come to be who and where you are now? Facilitator: Jonalu Johnstone

Spirituality Books: This covenant group meets monthly to talk about books that have a spiritual theme. Facilitator: Chris Lopez

—First Unitarian Church, Oklahoma City, Oklahoma

Sample Registration Form

Name _____

Address _____

City, State, Zip _____

Phone _____

E-mail _____

I am already a member of a Chalice Circle.

I wish to recommit to my present circle

I wish to switch to a different circle

I am unable to continue at this time

Comments:

I wish to join a Chalice Circle

I am available on the following days and times:
(circle all that apply)

Monday	morning	afternoon	evening
Tuesday	morning	afternoon	evening
Wednesday	morning	afternoon	evening
Thursday	morning	afternoon	evening
Friday	morning	afternoon	evening
Saturday	morning	afternoon	evening
Sunday	(none)	afternoon	evening

I have the following special need in order for me to be able to participate in a Chalice Circle.

Please return your form to the First Parish Office no later than Oct. 1.

—First Parish of Sudbury, Massachusetts

Sample Invitation to Potential Facilitators

You've heard about our exciting new Chalice Circle group program.
Have you considered being a facilitator?

Why?

Churches across the country have enthusiastically shared the opportunities and benefits provided by small group programs. *You* could be a part of bringing this cutting edge ministry to First Church! *You* could help provide important new avenues for the growth and spiritual development of both our individual members and for our church community overall! As we get our program off the ground we are seeking adventurous members such as yourself to consider applying to be our first facilitators.

Who?

Facilitators need to meet certain criteria including being a member of the congregation, being self-aware and willing to learn, being a good listener, being receptive and unprejudiced, and being comfortable in a group setting.

What would I need to do?

Facilitators will be expected to help set a tone of acceptance and respect for all members, to follow the established group format (e.g., starting each group with the lighting of the chalice and a check-in), to encourage each member to participate as they are willing, to intervene if the group needs redirection, and to coordinate or delegate the coordination of the business aspects of the group (e.g., When's the next meeting? Does someone want to bring a snack?).

Would I receive training?

Yes! The applicants selected will participate in five two-hour group training sessions modeling the Chalice Circle format and covering the topics of spirituality, leadership, and small group theory. Training sessions will occur at the church and are mandatory. The training dates to span five consecutive Tuesdays evenings (7:00-9:00) beginning on January 8 and running until February 5. Our trainers, Candice Haight and Robert Szymanski, are talented and experienced educators. In the final session they will invite trainees to evaluate whether they are still interested in making a commitment to the program.

What about ongoing support?

The monthly facilitator meetings are designed to offer ongoing support and assistance in helping you develop your skills and troubleshooting any difficulties that arise.

What's the time commitment?

Leading a small group would require attendance at Chalice Circle meetings once or twice monthly, in addition to monthly facilitator meetings. All of the meetings are two hours in duration. The day and time of your small group would be set at your convenience; the schedule for the facilitator meetings will be decided by the facilitator group. Groups are planned to launch in February of 2002 and we request facilitators to commit to serving their group through the next church year ending in May 2003. Whether groups continue to meet during the summer will be up to them.

You're interested?

Here's the next step . . . Pick up and complete an application form available at the Membership Table during coffee hour. Return the application by November 18th to the Member Services table or mail it to First Church "attn: Lisa Radtke." We hope to interview all applicants (if numbers permit) and plan to make final decisions by mid-December.

Although we realize we will be interviewing many qualified candidates we are restricted to selecting only eight individuals for this initial training. Those we are unable to select initially will be invited to participate in a group as a member or await the next facilitator training opportunity.

—First Unitarian Society of Milwaukee, Milwaukee, Wisconsin

Sample Facilitator's Application Form

1. What interests you in becoming a facilitator for a Chalice Circle group at First Church?

2. What skills/qualities do you possess which you think might be useful to you in the role of facilitator?

3. Please describe any prior small group experiences you have had, as facilitator or participant.

4. From what you know about the Chalice Circle groups, what do you hope they could do for you and for the church community at large?

5. What training do you believe you would need to be an effective facilitator?

6. Is there anything else you would like us to know, or that you think would be helpful for us to know as we consider you for this position?

Thank you very much for your interest in the Chalice Circle group program.

Application deadline: November 18, 2001. Applications may be turned into the Member Services Table on Sunday morning, or send to the church office marked "Attention: Lisa Radtke."

Name: _____

Phone: day _____   eve _____

—First Unitarian Society of Milwaukee, Wisconsin

Sample Facilitator's Training Session

Reading, Chalice Lighting, and Silence

Check-In: Why do you want to be a covenant group leader?

Review Agenda

History & Development of Covenant Groups

Purpose of Covenant Groups

- To provide a sense of intimacy and community for people.
  That's why we shoot for the magic number of ten people involved in a group. It's simply the maximum number which experience has shown can sustain the intimacy needed to meet people's needs. Go beyond that and there is less participation and more burnout on the part of the leaders. If you go beyond ten you have a class rather than a relational group.
- The groups provide a place for spiritual exploration and growth.
  In an environment where people are encouraged and supported in the sharing of stories, experiences, ideas and feelings, they are able to develop spiritually.
- The groups are encouraged to commit themselves to reaching out to the church and community.
- Groups are challenged to provide the opportunity for others to be involved by helping to create more covenant groups. Groups are also asked to take responsibility for a project in the church or community, such as volunteering to put on Coffee Hour together on a Sunday morning or working together on a Habitat for Humanity home. Participants are asked to invite friends to their group, whether they are members or not.

The Covenant Group Process

Opening Reading and Chalice Lighting followed by period of silence (this responsibility is moved around the group)

Check-in: About yourself, your day, your high and low since the last meeting

Group discussion: The group facilitator chooses an overall topic that he/she is passionate about, but the group can decide where to go with it.

Check-out: Brief feedback about the meeting, what people liked, what they would change.

Closing reading

Facilitator Job Description

- Commit to organize and facilitate a covenant group of up to 10 people for a year.

  - Decide what kind of group you want to lead, how often, and location, and then advertise for members in the *Arlingtarian.*
  - Take care of mechanics by making sure things are assigned and done. Have an opening and closing reading in hand.
  - Facilitate a good discussion and help keep the group on task, model good process and listening skills, and help the group adhere to their own covenants with each other about behavior, including starting the meetings on time and ending on time.
  - Don't conduct a meeting or teach or do therapy and don't lead too much. Remember that it is the members who "own" the group and have the primary responsibility for its success or failure.

- Train a cofacilitator by choosing someone in the group who you believe will make a good facilitator and ask that person to cofacilitate and train with you. After each meeting go over the process with the cofacilitator. When the group divides the cofacilitator will lead the second group.
- Meet with the ministers in a covenant group on a regular basis.

Questions & Discussion

Check-Out

Closing Reading

—Unitarian Universalist Church, Arlington, Virginia

Sample Covenanting Process

1. Participants write the answers to two questions on cards in each of the first three sessions.

    *   What do I hope to bring from my life to the group?
    *   What do I hope to take from the group to my life?

    Answers are read aloud, either by the leader or the participants.

2. Leader types up the answers and distributes the lists in session four.
3. Using a flip chart and with the assistance of the facilitator, the group writes a covenant statement.

Note: Many facilitators are afraid. (What if we can't write one or it's inadequate?) This process can be a little scary at first even for those with experience and training in facilitation. You just have to have faith that a good covenant will emerge. When it does the groups are very proud of their statements, even a little euphoric.

—Unitarian Church, Baton Rouge, Louisiana

Resources

Books and Tapes, General

Andrews, Cecile. *The Circle of Simplicity: Return to the Good Life.* New York: Harper-Collins, 1997.

Corrigan, Thom, and Richard Pearce. *Learning to Care: Developing Community in Small Groups.* Colorado Springs, CO: Pilgrimage/NavPress, 1997.

Davis, Deena, ed. *Discipleship Journal's 101 Best Small-Group Ideas.* Colorado Springs, CO: NavPress, 1996.

Donahue, Bill. *The Willow Creek Guide to Leading Life-Changing Small Groups.* Grand Rapids, MI: Zondervan, 1996.

George, Carl. *The Coming Church Revolution.* Grand Rapids, MI: Revell, 1991.

———. *How to Break Growth Barriers.* Grand Rapids, MI: Baker House, 1993.

———. *Nine Keys to Effective Small Group Leadership.* Mansfield, PA: Kingdom Publishing, 1997.

———. *Prepare Your Church for the Future.* Grand Rapids, MI: Revell, 1991.

Hudgens, A. Gayle. *Collaborative Spunk: The Feisty Guide for Reviving People and Our Planet.* Helena, MT: SOS Press, 2002.

Hunter, Dale, Anne Bailey, and Bill Taylor. *The Art of Facilitation.* Cambridge, MA: Fisher Books, 1995.

Kouzes, James M., and Barry Z. Posner. *Encouraging the Heart: A Leader's Guide to Rewarding and Recognizing Others.* San Francisco: Jossey Bass, 1999.

McBride, Neal F. *How to Build a Small-Groups Ministry.* Colorado Springs, CO: Navpress, 1995.

Ray, Paul H. *The Integral Culture Survey: A Study of the Emergence of Transformational Values in America.* Sausalito, CA: Institute of Noetic Sciences, and Kalamazoo, MI: Fetzer Institute, 1993.

Ray, Paul H., and Sherry Ruth Anderson. *The Cultural Creatives: How 50 Million People Are Shaping the World.* New York: Harmony Books, 2000. (For more on cultural creatives, see www.culturalcreatives.org.)

Thandeka. *Engagement Groups: Bringing Forth the Future from the Past.* London: Lindsey Press, 2002.

——. *"The Spiritual Life of Unitarian Universalists, Lost and Found," A Global Conversation: Unitarian/Universalism at the Dawn of the 21st Century.* Edited by Andrew M. Hill, Jill K. McAllister, and Clifford M. Reed. Prague: International Council of Unitarians and Universalists, 2002.

Turner, Nathan. *Leading Small Groups.* Valley Forge, PA: Judson Press, 1996.

Ward, Allan. *Beyond the Visible Spectrum.* Little Rock, AR: Award Press, 2002.

Wuthnow, Robert. *Sharing the Journey: Support Groups and America's New Quest for Community.* New York: Free Press, 1994.

——, ed. *"I Came Away Stronger": How Small Groups Are Shaping American Religion.* Grand Rapids, MI: Eerdmans, 1994.

Printed Materials Specific to Unitarian Universalism

Fry, Christine, et al. *Good Life Covenant Group: A Resource Guide, 2001–2002.* Davis, CA: Unitarian Universalist Church, 2000. Available from Unitarian Universalist Church, 27074 Patwin Rd., Davis, CA 95616–9720.

Hamilton-Holway, Barbara. *Evensong: An Eight-Week Series of Gatherings.* Boston: Skinner House Books, 2001.

———. *Evensong, Volume 2: An Eight-Week Series of Gatherings.* Boston: Skinner House Books, 2002.

Herz, Walter P., ed. *Redeeming Time: Endowing Your Church with the Power of the Covenant.* Boston: Skinner House Books, 1998.

Morgan, John. *The Devotional Heart: Pietism and the Renewal of American Unitarian Universalism.* Boston: Skinner House Books, 1995.

Phillips, Roy D. *Transforming Liberal Congregations for the New Millennium.* St. Paul: Unity Church, Unitarian, 1996.

Smith Valley, Judith. "The Small Group Ministry Project of the First Parish Unitarian Universalist Church Kennebunk, Maine." Ph.D. diss., Bangor Theological Seminary, 2001.

Resources Available On-line or by E-mail

Bowden, Peter. *Peter's Small Group News.* A small group ministry newsletter available at http://www.smallgroupministry.net/.

Bumbaugh, David. "A Contemporary Assessment of Unitarian Universalism." *Journal of Liberal Religion* 3, no. 2 (2002). Available at http://www.meadville.edu/ in the "Journal" section.

Cavenaugh, Rob. *Rob's Covenant Group Manual.* Available from the author at RCavenaugh@uua.org.

Center for Community Values. *Covenant Group Source Book.* Chicago: CCV, 2000. Available from the Center for Community Values, 1507 E. 53rd St. #901, Chicago, IL 60615, or http://www.the-ccv.org.

Dame, Calvin. *A Small Group Ministry Resource Book.* "Session Questions" and other materials available from the Unitarian Universalist Community Church, 69 Winthrop St., Augusta, ME 04330–5505, or http://home.gwi.net/~uuccaug/sgm.htm.

Hill, Robert L., ed. *Covenant Group News.* Available at www.swuuc.org in the "Programs" section.

Turner, Glenn H. *Designing and Implementing a Small Group Ministry Focus for Your Congregation.* Available from the Unitarian Universalist Community Church, 69 Winthrop St., Augusta, ME 04330–5505, or http://home.gwi.net/~uuccaug/sgm. htm.

———. "Transforming Our Churches With Small Group Ministry." *Journal of Liberal Religion* 1, no. 2 (2000). Available at http://www.meadville.edu/ in the "Journal" section.

Unitarian Universalist Association. Discussion of small group ministry issues available at http://www.uua.org/mailman/listinfo/covenant_group_ministry. A search for "Covenant Groups" at www.uua.org will produce additional resources as they are added.

Zidowecki, Helen. *Small Group Ministry and Religious Education.* Available at www.hzmre.com in the "Small Group Ministry" section.